The Adventures of
Dylan

D1148626

The Adventures of
Dylan

Eric Thompson

The stories of *The Magic Roundabout*

Originally created by Serge Danot
in a series entitled *Le Manège Enchanté*

BLOOMSBURY

IN THE SAME SERIES

THE ADVENTURES OF DOUGAL
THE ADVENTURES OF ERMINTRUDE
THE ADVENTURES OF BRIAN

First published in 1998

Copyright © Eric Thompson 1968–1975
Copyright © Serge Danot/AB Productions SA
Licensed by Link Licensing

Bloomsbury Publishing Plc, 38 Soho Square, London W1V 5DF

All rights reserved. Without limiting the rights under copyright reserved above, no part of this publication may be reproduced, stored in or introduced into a retrieval system, or transmitted, in any form or by any means (electronic, mechanical, photocopying, recording or otherwise), without the prior written permission of both the copyright owners and the above publisher of this book.

A CIP catalogue record for this book is available from the British Library

10 9 8 7 6 5 4 3 2

ISBN 0 7475 4252 X

Typeset by Dorchester Typesetting Group Ltd
Printed in Great Britain by Clays Ltd, St Ives plc

These stories are transcripts of the *Magic Roundabout* TV series that appeared on television in the late sixties and early seventies, as narrated and written by Eric Thompson.

Dylan Decides to Stay a While

Florence told Zebedee that she wasn't able to go to the garden because she had to practise the piano at home.

'Very laudable,' said Zebedee, 'but it just so happens there's something to be learned about music in the garden today.'

'What can you mean?' said Florence.

'Go and see,' said Zebedee, casually.

'All right, I will,' said Florence, 'and I'll practise tomorrow – very hard.'

When Florence got to the garden she found it was very hot. She asked Dougal if he found it hot.

'Swel-ter-ing!' said Dougal.

'Take your coat off,' said Florence.

'Very funny,' said Dougal.

'We need a fan,' said Florence.

'I beg your pardon?' said Dougal.

'We need a fan,' said Florence, 'to fan ourselves with.' And she looked around and noticed some very long leaves. 'Let's make a fan out of leaves,' said Florence, and she went to pick some.

'You do have some funny ideas,' said Dougal, 'but you're very clever.'

And he went to help.

So they picked some leaves to make a fan.

'That's lovely,' said Florence.

'Just a few more,' muttered Dougal. 'Oh, they seem to be stuck . . . um . . . hm . . . oh dear . . .'

Just then, strangely enough, a stranger arrives.

'Steady, man,' said the stranger. 'Steady . . .'

'Good heavens,' said Dougal.

'Interested in nature, man?' said the stranger.

'Er . . . whom do I have the honour of addressing?' said Dougal.

'Name's Dylan, man,' said the stranger. 'I'm a rabbit.'

'You could have fooled me,' said Dougal.

'I just arrived in your pleasant garden. Think I might, like . . . stay a while . . .'

'My name's Dougal,' said Dougal, 'and this is . . . er . . . Miss Florence.'

'Glad to know you, mam,' said Dylan.

'Glad to know *you*,' said Florence.

'He's a rabbit,' said Dougal.

'How interesting,' said Florence, politely.

'We just arrived – me and my guitar,' said Dylan.

'You play the guitar?' said Florence.

'Like a dream,' said Dylan, and he went to get it.

'What's his name?' whispered Florence.

'Dylan,' hissed Dougal.

Dylan returns humming.

'Here we are,' said Dylan. 'Like . . . the group

complete.'

'Would you play us a tune?' said Florence.

But Dylan said that before playing he had to find inspiration and relaxation.

'Do you read music?' said Florence.

'No, I play by ear, mam,' said Dylan.

'Well, they're big enough,' said Dougal to himself. 'Hee! Hee!'

'Quiet please,' said Dylan.

Dylan plays some chords.

'That's lovely,' said Florence.

'Play "Scotland the Brave",' said Dougal.

And Dylan asked him to write it down as he didn't know it.

'You don't know "Scotland the Brave"?!' said Dougal.

Dougal hums it, petering out after a few notes.

'Don't know it?' said Dougal.

'What label's it on?' said Dylan.

We've got a right one here, thought Dougal.

'Play something else, Dylan,' said Florence.

'Inspiration's gone,' said Dylan.

'Oh, I am sorry,' said Florence.

And Dylan's inspiration was so far gone – he fell asleep.

'He's asleep!' said Florence.

'What a funny rabbit,' said Dougal, and he played a

note on the guitar, which woke Dylan up.

'Do I hear music?' said Dylan.

'Er . . . no!' said Dougal.

But Dylan's sleep had given him inspiration . . .

Dylan plays and hums, inspired.

'Gone, man, gone,' said Dylan.

'He's gone again,' said Florence.

And he had.

'The effort was too much for him,' said Dougal.

So Florence and Dougal decided they had better leave Dylan to gather his inspiration, and they left, very quietly.

'Goodbye, Dougal,' whispered Florence.

'Goodbye, Florence,' whispered Dougal, giggling.

And when Zebedee arrived, he asked Florence if she'd learned anything about music.

'It was most instructive,' said Florence, thoughtfully. 'Good-night, Dougal.'

A Vacant Pad

Florence was waiting, as usual, and when Zebedee arrived she told him she was going to see Dougal.

'Dougal *is* lucky,' said Zebedee.

'Why?' said Florence.

'You're his friend,' said Zebedee.

'Thank you,' said Florence.

Florence asked Dougal what he would like to do, and Dougal thought . . .

'You decide,' he said. 'We'll do what you want to do.'

'Let's go for a walk,' said Florence.

'Oh, ha! Ha! Lovely!' said Dougal. 'Hum!'

'It'll do you good,' said Florence.

'That's what my mother used to say,' said Dougal.

Dylan had decided he liked the garden and was looking for a place to stay.

'Like . . . a vacant pad!' he said to himself – and he got into Dougal's bed.

But he found he had company . . .

'Per-lease!' said Brian.

'Do you mind!' said Brian.

'Who are *you*?' said Brian.

'Name's Dylan,' said Dylan. 'Is this your place?'

'Er . . . no,' said Brian. 'No.'

And Dylan explained that he was looking for a place to live.

'Well, this bed belongs to my old mate Dougal,' said Brian.

'Dougal?' said Dylan. 'Isn't that that crazy dog with the . . . like . . .way-out fur?'

'Yes, it is!' said Brian.

'We're old friends,' said Dylan. 'Buddies . . .'

'Then make yourself at home,' said Brian. 'I'm *sure* he won't mind.'

So Dylan made himself at home . . .

He grunts, sighs, falls asleep and snores.

And Brian, sniggering, just thought he would go and find Dougal.

Meanwhile . . .

'Enjoying your walk?' asked Florence, happily.

'Lovely!' said Dougal, heavily. 'Hello, mollusc.'

'Hello! Hello! Hello!' said Brian.

'Where're you going?' said Brian, casually.

'We're going to my place,' said Dougal.

'Want to come?' said Florence.

'I've just been,' said Brian. 'Hum. Er . . . there's a friend of yours there,' he said.

'A friend of mine?' said Dougal.

'Yes – in your bed,' said Brian.

'In my bed?!' said Dougal.

'In your bed!' said Brian.

'I can't recall inviting anyone,' said Dougal. 'Come,

Florence.'

And they went.

'What fun!' said Brian, giggling.

'I wonder who it is,' said Florence.

'I *wonder*,' said Dougal, grimly.

And then they found out. 'It's that *rabbit*,' said Dougal.

'Yes, it is,' said Florence.

'I *knew* we'd have trouble with this one,' said Dougal.

'Sh!' said Florence. 'You'll wake him up.'

'That's the idea,' said Dougal, and he prepared to shout very loud.

'I don't think you should wake him,' said Florence. 'Think of his inspiration.'

'I'll inspire him,' said Dougal.

Dougal plays an inspired discord on Dylan's guitar.

'Do I hear music?' said Dylan, yawning.

'Yes, you do!' said Dougal.

'You play by nose, man?' said Dylan.

'You keep my nose out of this, sir,' said Dougal.

'Gladly, man, gladly,' said Dylan.

'You are in my bed, sir,' said Dougal.

'And very comfortable,' said Dylan.

'Please get out,' said Dougal.

'Why should I, man?' said Dylan, and Florence saw trouble ahead . . .

'It's not your bed, Dylan,' she said, 'it's Dougal's.'

'People have been put in pies for less,' said Dougal.

And Florence thought they were both behaving badly

– and told them so. And Dylan told them he was sorry and could he have his guitar back?

'Not till you get off my bed,' said Dougal.

'I think you're both being very difficult,' said Florence.

But she gave Dylan his guitar back and Dougal got his bed back.

'Now, be friends,' said Florence. 'I know it's difficult – but try.'

'Rabbits and dogs never could get on,' said Zebedee. 'Time for bed . . .'

Cutting the Grass

Dylan was playing his guitar quietly to himself.

But he found that playing his guitar close to the ground, the grass tended to get caught in the strings. It was against Dylan's nature to stand up to play, so he thought of another solution. He would cut the grass.

Dylan starts up a lawnmower, which, as lawnmowers tend to be, is rather noisy and clackety.

'Like . . . a lawnmower,' he said. 'Crazy.'

'What! What! What! What's that?! Am I being attacked? The natives are rising. What?! What!' said Dougal.

Dougal got a little confused, and then he thought it must be an aeroplane about to crash . . .

'Don't crash on me!' he shouted.

And he told Zebedee to take cover.

'There's an aeroplane about to crash!' he said.

'Really?' said Zebedee.

'Don't just stand there,' said Dougal.

But Zebedee told him it was just the sound of a lawnmower.

'A lawnmower?' said Dougal.

'Dylan's cutting the grass, I think,' said Zebedee.

'What?!' said Dougal. 'That rabbit working? You

must be dotty! He's never done a day's work in his life.
It's an aeroplane! Oh dear! Oh dear!'

Zebedee tried to calm Dougal down . . .

'IT'S A LAWNMOWER!' he shouted.

'There's no need to shout,' said Dougal.

'Sorry,' said Zebedee.

'It's an aeroplane,' said Dougal, quietly.

So Zebedee went to see Florence to see if she could
persuade Dougal that aeroplanes weren't crashing all
around him.

'He's got a bee in his bonnet,' said Zebedee.

'He usually has,' said Florence.

And she goes to the garden to see what she can do.

She asked Dougal what was going on.

'You may well ask,' said Dougal, 'with planes crashing all around and the garden in flames and chaos.'

'I don't see any chaos,' said Florence, 'or flames.'

'It's only a matter of time,' said Dougal. 'Can't you
hear it? It'll crash any moment.'

'Sounds like a lawnmower to me,' said Florence.

Meanwhile, Dylan mowed on, and Dougal still
believed it was an aeroplane – crashing.

'There you are!' said Florence. 'A lawnmower!'

'I'm not convinced,' said Dougal. 'It could be a *small*
aeroplane . . . and the noise has stopped!'

'What's that prove?' said Florence.

'It proves it's crashed,' said Dougal. 'It has all the
characteristics of a light aircraft,' he muttered.

'This is a lawn, man, not an airstrip,' yawned Dylan.

'Have a good sleep?' said Florence.

'Thank you, mam, yes,' said Dylan with a yawn. 'I feel wide awake.'

Just then Brian came along and wanted to know what everyone was *doing*.

'I thought I heard a noise like an aeroplane,' he said, innocently.

'It *was* an aeroplane,' said Dougal triumphantly, 'and here it is!'

'Looks like a lawnmower to me,' said Brian.

'You've got lawnmowers on the brain – all of you,' said Dougal.

'Oh, we are in a mood, aren't we?' said Brian, not too loudly.

And Florence tried to think of a way to prove that it *was* a lawnmower and not a crashed aeroplane.

'Best of luck, mam,' said Dylan, and he left.

And Zebedee, when he heard all about it, said, 'If it's an aeroplane, where's the pilot?'

'Don't bother me with details,' said Dougal.

Florence sighed . . . and Zebedee sighed . . . because once Dougal got an idea it was difficult to get him out of it.

'If it's an aeroplane, where's its wings?' said Brian, loudly.

'Wings? Wings?' said Dougal. 'Oh, wings? Hum. Foolish mollusc . . . whoever heard of a lawnmower with wings. Ha! Ha!'

'Time for bed,' sighed Zebedee.

A Certain Smell

Dougal was in the garden when he noticed something.

'What's this?' said Dougal, sniffing. 'What's this? Scent? Perfume?'

He asked Zebedee if he noticed anything.

'No,' said Zebedee.

'Not a . . . *je ne sais pas* . . . a certain *smell* in the air?' said Dougal.

'No, I don't,' said Zebedee.

'Of course I realise you lack my delicate dog's sense of smell, but surely you catch a breath of something?' said Dougal.

'No,' said Zebedee.

'Nose not working?' said Dougal.

'Never has worked,' said Zebedee.

'Really?' said Dougal.

'Really,' said Zebedee.

'Well,' said Dougal, 'someone is making scent in the garden – the smell is *very* strong.'

'I'll ask Florence,' said Zebedee.

'Ask her . . .' said Dougal.

'Yes?' said Zebedee.

'Ask her if she prefers English lavender or Scottish heather for perfume, will you?' said Dougal.

'English lavender or Scottish heather. All right,' said Zebedee, leaving.

'English lavender or Scottish heather?' muttered Zebedee.

'I beg your pardon?' said Florence.

So Zebedee told Florence all about the scent . . . and Mr Rusty said *he'd* noticed a sort of smell about the garden too.

'Someone must be making perfume,' said Zebedee.

'Who could it be?' said Florence.

'You'd better go and find out, hadn't you?' said Zebedee.

'Yes, I'd better,' said Florence.

'Dougal will help you with his sensitive nose,' said Zebedee.

'And bring me a bottle of lavender water,' said Mr Rusty. 'It's my favourite.'

'All right,' said Florence, and away she went.

Dougal met Dylan. 'May I ask a question?' said Dougal.

'Be my guest,' said Dylan.

'Aren't rabbits supposed to be bouncy?' said Dougal.

'I'm starting a new trend,' said Dylan.

'Oh, I see,' said Dougal.

'We're rethinking the image,' said Dylan.

So Dougal asked Dylan if he smelled anything.

'Like carrot stew?' said Dylan.

'Not exactly,' said Dougal, 'more like violets and heather.'

'Oh, brother!' said Dylan and went on his way.

Florence asked Dougal if he knew where the scent was coming from and Dougal said he didn't, so they decided to try and find it. They looked . . . and sniffed. . .

'I think we're getting warmer,' said Florence.

'Well, it's certainly getting smellier,' said Dougal.

'It's a pity you're not a bloodhound, Dougal,' said Florence.

'Huh! Great floppy things!' said Dougal. He gave another sniff. 'Ah! Ha! I believe we've found it.'

'We might have known,' said Florence.

They stop outside Mr MacHenry's greenhouse.

And of course Florence was right – who else would make perfume in the garden but Mr MacHenry?

'Nice smell, Mr MacHenry,' they said.

'Glad you like it,' said Mr MacHenry.

'Is it English lavender?' said Florence.

'And Scottish heather,' said Mr MacHenry.

'Both?!' said Florence.

'Both!' said Mr MacHenry.

'I'm not sure the clans are going to like this,' said Dougal.

'It's a *lovely* scent,' said Florence.

'That's not what I meant,' said Dougal. 'Haven't got any essence of sugar, have you?'

'Oh, Dougal! You!' said Florence – but Mr MacHenry had gone anyway.

And Florence told Zebedee all about it.

'Did you remember Mr Rusty's lavender water?' said Zebedee.

'No,' said Florence.

'Perhaps I'll make some essence of sugar tomorrow,' mused Dougal. 'Good-night.'

No work, No beans

Mr MacHenry was sorting out his plans for sowing seeds in the garden. He had some special seeds he wanted to try out and he was just wondering where to put them.

Now where? he thought.

Zebedee asked him what he was doing.

'Sowing seeds,' said Mr MacHenry and Zebedee told him that *he* had some special seeds too.

'Look!' he said. 'Look . . .'

A jumping bean appears and starts to grow.

'You have green fingers, my friend,' said Mr MacHenry.

'That and a little magic,' said Zebedee, happily. 'You have to have a little magic.'

'All seeds are a bit magical, I always think,' said Mr MacHenry, mystically.

More jumping beans appear.

Dylan came along to see what was happening.

'What's the scene, man?' he said.

Mr MacHenry decided to pick the beans before it rained and he asked Dylan to help.

'Work, man?' said Dylan. 'You want to give me bad

dreams? Let it rain – real coool!'

'Lazy thing,' said Mr MacHenry.

But Dylan said he wasn't lazy – he loved work – he could look at it for hours (and had done so, often), but he said he wouldn't mind a few beans to eat.

'No work – no beans,' said Dylan, sadly. 'Story of my life, man, story of my life.'

And after looking at the beans again he left.

'Like, goodbye,' he said.

Mr MacHenry sighed. 'Youth! Youth!' he said.

And he was just wondering what to do about the jumping beans when Dougal came along.

'Mercy on us! Fleas!' screamed Dougal. 'Help! Assistance! Aid! Keep them off! Fleas!'

Mr MacHenry tried to explain but Dougal was not going to risk being invaded, so he left.

Zebedee told Florence about the beans and how Mr MacHenry was afraid it would snow and spoil them.

'Couldn't you do some magic?' said Florence.

And Zebedee said he probably *could* if he was put to it, so he thought . . . And Florence thought . . . And Zebedee finally decided that if it was going to rain, or snow, or hail the beans should be protected in some way.

'What a good idea,' said Florence. 'Goodbye.'

So Zebedee put the beans under glass.

'What a good idea,' said Mr MacHenry.

And Dylan said he would go to sleep near the beans.

'In case they jump,' he said, 'I'll go to sleep with my mouth, like, open, man.'

Party Time

Florence had told Dougal to fetch Dylan as they were all going on a trip with Zebedee, but with a rabbit like Dylan fetching wasn't very easy . . .

'Party time,' said Dougal.

'Oh, brother!' said Dylan, yawning.

'I shall never understand you,' said Dougal. 'Rabbits are supposed to leap about and do jolly things – didn't they tell you?'

'Oh, they told me,' said Dylan, yawning again, 'but I didn't dig . . .'

And he went to sleep again.

'Everyone ready?' said Zebedee.

'Well *I'm* ready,' said Dougal. 'I don't guarantee anyone else.'

But Dylan said that he was quite ready and wanted to come. So Zebedee said he would just get Florence and then they could go.

'Are Dougal and Dylan coming?' said Florence.

'Eventually,' said Zebedee.

'Is Dylan awake?' said Florence.

'Just about,' said Zebedee.

So they started out to see what they could see.

Florence asked Zebedee where they were going.

'It's a surprise,' said Zebedee.

'Is it far?' said Dylan.

'Tired *already*?' said Dougal.

But Dylan said he'd go on and wait for them.

'I'll never understand rabbits,' said Dougal.

'He'll never understand rabbits,' said Dylan.

'*Is* it far?' said Florence.

And Zebedee said it wasn't.

Very soon, they arrive at a windmill.

And it wasn't far. He had brought them to see the windmills.

'Windmills!' said Florence.

'*Wind*mills?!' said Dougal.

Dougal spies a waterwheel.

'And water-mills!' said Dougal. 'Grinding any sugar today?'

But the water-mill said he didn't grind sugar – only corn.

'I must introduce you to a rabbit I know,' said Dougal.

Florence was talking to a windmill. 'What do you do if the wind doesn't blow?' she said.

'Go to sleep,' said the windmill.

'I must introduce you to a rabbit I know,' said Dougal.

Florence thought all the different mills were lovely.

'Do *you* grind sugar?' said Dougal, hopefully.

Suddenly, they heard something . . .

'ATISHOO! ATISHOO!'

'What's that?' said Florence.

'Sounds like someone with a cold,' said Dougal.

'ATISHOO! ATISHOO!'

'Yes, it does,' said Florence.

But then they saw . . . it was a *pepper-mill.*

'A pepper-mill!' said Florence.

'Got a cold?' said Dougal.

'Doh!' said the pepper-mill, nasally. 'It's just that pepper doesn't agree with me. ATISHOO!'

'Oh, poor thing,' said Florence.

'He'll have to get another job,' said Dougal. 'Like sugar grinding.'

Then they realised that Dylan was nowhere to be seen, so they went to look for him.

'This is becoming a bit of a joke,' said Dougal. 'Enjoying yourself?' he said loudly.

'Wild, man,' said Dylan, yawning sleepily.

'Did you like the windmills?' said Dougal.

'What windmills?' said Dylan.

'You really must try and *participate* more,' said Florence.

'Yes, and join in more too,' said Dougal.

'I *protest*,' said Dylan.

Florence thanked Zebedee very much for showing them his mills. 'I suppose it's time for bed now,' she said.

'I know a certain rabbit who'll be glad to hear it,' said Dougal. 'Ha! Ha!'

Night-time Jumping

Dougal found Dylan fast asleep with his mouth open – and snoring. This disturbed Dougal's sensibility and he decided that it must not go on.

'Nice day!' he shouted, and Dylan woke up.

'Nice day,' said Dougal, chattily.

'Oh, man!' said Dylan.

'You had your mouth open,' said Dougal.

'For a reason, cookie,' said Dylan.

'What reason?' said Dougal.

And Dylan explained about the jumping beans and how he slept with his mouth open in case they jumped up.

'That's lazy, Dylan,' said Dougal.

'That's sense, man,' said Dylan.

Dougal looked at the beans. 'They look like fleas to me,' he said.

'I don't eat fleas,' said Dylan.

'They jump, do they?' said Dougal.

'That's it, man,' said Dylan. 'And if I've got my mouth open then – Boing! Boing!'

'Haven't got any jumping sugar, have you?' said Dougal.

But Dylan said that he didn't have any jumping sugar.

'Pity,' said Dougal.

The beans start jumping. Boing! Boing!

And suddenly there was Zebedee. 'How are the beans?' he said.

'Jumping, man, jumping,' said Dylan.

And Zebedee got very interested in the beans . . . and so did Dylan . . . and so did Dougal. So interested, in fact, that they forgot they were to meet Florence. But Florence didn't mind waiting – at least she *said* she didn't.

'So sorry,' murmured Zebedee.

Meanwhile, the beans continued to amuse . . .

'What are they?' said Florence.

'Beans, man,' said Dylan.

'She's not a man,' said Dougal.

'Do they do that all the time?' said Florence.

'No,' said Mr MacHenry. 'Not all the time. They only jump when it's light. Don't jump in the dark – well-known fact.'

Dylan looked sad.

'What's the matter?' said Florence.

And Dylan explained that as the beans only jumped when it was light and it always seemed to be dark when he was asleep, he'd never get any beans to eat.

'Ah well,' he sighed, 'back to the carrots, man.'

'Find some jumping carrots, man,' said Dougal.

'Carrots are very good for you,' said Florence. 'Even if they aren't as interesting as jumping beans.'

And she asked Zebedee if she could take some of the beans to show the others.

'Of course,' said Zebedee.

'You're very kind,' said Florence.

The Lettuce Thief

Brian was very agitated (an awesome sight).

'You seem a bit agitated,' said Dougal.

'I am *very* agitated,' said Brian.

'Tell me why, little creature,' said Dougal. 'I have moments to spare.'

So Brian told Dougal that he had seen Dylan picking lettuces. 'Out of my garden,' he said. 'My best lettuces – my best – grown and nurtured for weeks. It's not right! I call on you, an upright dog, to help the weak. Namely me.'

And he described how he had seen Dylan pick the lettuces. He'd seen him look at them closely. He'd seen him put the lettuces in a basket. And steal away . . .

'I saw him! I saw him!' said Brian.

'We must be careful not to rush to conclusions,' said Dougal. 'We must go and investigate. Come, Watson.'

'Watson?' said Brian.

So they went to see . . . and it seemed that Brian was right.

'It seems you were right,' hissed Dougal.

'I know I'm right,' hissed Brian.

'Leave this to me,' said Dougal.

'Gladly, old strong friend,' said Brian.

So they went to see Dylan . . .

'Greetings, greetings, man and man,' said Dylan.

'Ha hum!' said Dougal.

'Bite him!' said Brian.

The children came to see what the matter was . . .

'*Now-own-up*,' said Dougal.

'Own up!' said Florence.

'Own up?' said the boy. 'Own up?'

'Up to what?' said the girl.

'Don't impede the investigation, please,' said Dougal.

'What investigation?' said Zebedee, and everyone shouted to speak at once.

And as Florence explained no one seemed to know what was going on except Brian and Dougal.

'It's an open and shut case,' said Dougal, loudly.

'An open and shut case,' said Brian.

But Dylan explained that he had picked the lettuces to wash them, because they looked dirty.

'The lettuces were dirty?' said Florence. 'And you wanted to wash them?'

'I abhor a dirty lettuce,' said Dylan, yawning.

'But were they *your* lettuces?' said Florence.

'No, they were mine!' said Brian. 'And they weren't *very* dirty, just a bit grubby. I like them a bit grubby.'

'Steady, Brian,' said Florence soothingly. 'He *did* plant them again.'

'Yes, in his *own* garden,' said Brian, beside himself with fury . . .

But Zebedee said that everything in the garden belonged to everyone – which was quite right and proper.

'Cool common property, man,' said Dylan. 'Lettuces belong to the people.'

'And the people are welcome to them,' said Dougal. 'Don't go washing any sugar, will you?'

'It's an idea, man,' said Dylan. 'I'll put my mind to it.' And he left.

'He can't mean it,' said Dougal. 'Can he?'

A Good Day's Sleep

Dylan asked Mr MacHenry what he was growing and Mr MacHenry told him it was cotton.

'Cotton?' said Dylan.

'Cotton,' said Mr MacHenry.

'Crazy,' said Dylan.

'Quite a good crop,' said Mr MacHenry.

'It looks . . . like . . . very soft,' said Dylan.

'It is soft,' said Mr MacHenry.

And Dylan, who was always looking for soft things to sleep on, asked Mr MacHenry if he could have some. And Mr MacHenry said he could, so Dylan went to look for something to put the cotton in, and Mr MacHenry went to count his carrots, just in case. And Dylan, who could work quite hard when his comfort was involved, started picking.

After working particularly hard, Dylan lies down.

'Crazy!' said Dylan, yawning.

'Good morning!' said Dougal, brightly.

'You got something to communicate?' said Dylan, yawning again.

'No! No!' said Dougal. 'Just passing the time of day.'

Dougal hums.

'What's that you're sleeping on?' said Dougal.

And Dylan explained it was a cotton mattress.

'Cotton?' said Dougal. 'Cotton? How very quaint. Ha! Ha! Never heard of springs?'

'Springs, man?' said Dylan.

'Springs!' said Dougal. '*Interior* springs in the . . . er . . . interior. That's what *you* want – busy sleeper like you.'

'Sounds like a fun idea,' said Dylan.

And Dougal said that he would get Dylan some springs to try.

'Have a little sleep while you're waiting,' he said. 'Ha! Ha!'

Dougal goes to Zebedee's house and takes his springs.

And Dylan tried Dougal's spring mattress and found it even better than cotton.

'Ho! Ho!' said Dougal.

'Funny thing,' said Zebedee. 'I've lost all my springs. Haven't seen them by any chance, have you?'

'Um . . . yes, I did see them somewhere,' said Dougal. 'Let me think . . .'

'Think hard,' said Zebedee, grimly. 'Springs – curly things that go "boing".'

'Spring mattresses are the greatest – the greatest,' yawned Dylan.

'Spring mattress?' said Zebedee, slowly. 'Spr-ing

matt-ress?'

He looked at Dougal.

'Ha! Ha! Ha!' said Dougal. 'Hum . . . I didn't think you used them,' he said.

'My stock in trade,' said Zebedee.

And Dylan decided he would go somewhere a little quieter to sleep.

'Like . . . goodbye,' he said, and he left the mattress behind.

'Er . . . seen Florence?' said Dougal.

'Florence!' said Zebedee. 'Too late! I must send her a telegram! She'll be worrying . . .'

'"Sorry, can't come. No springs. What's the weather like? Love Zebedee." What's the weather like?!' said Florence.

The Competition

Florence told Zebedee she was going to see a competition in the garden.

'What competition?' said Zebedee.

'Between Dougal and Dylan,' said Florence. 'To see who's best.'

'At sleeping?' asked Zebedee.

'No, long-jumping,' said Florence.

Dougal and Dylan were talking about their long-jump competition.

'We must have a judge,' said Dougal. 'Like the Olympic games.'

'We don't need a judge,' said Dylan.

'I'm sorry,' said Dougal, 'but if a thing's worth doing it's worth doing properly . . .'

'Hello, hello,' said Brian, and seeing him Dougal had an idea.

'Hello, hello, hello!' said Brian.

'We want you to be judge,' said Dougal. 'Say you're a judge!!' he whispered.

'I'm a judge!' said Brian. 'Why?' he whispered.

'Do as you're told!' hissed Dougal.

And he told Brian that he should measure the length of the jumps, and he showed him how to do it.

Dylan looked rather amused and very confident.

'Just remember,' whispered Dougal. 'I'll tell you what to say – all right?'

'All right, old thing,' said Brian.

Dylan said Dougal should jump first and Dougal said he didn't mind jumping first, so he did . . .

And Brian measured the distance.

'Er . . . two feet six inches,' he said.

'I'm conserving my strength,' said Dougal.

'Your go, Dylan,' said Brian.

So Dylan had a go . . .

'I think he's in orbit,' said Brian.

'Listen,' said Dougal, as he whispered in Brian's ear.

'Yes, all right,' said Brian.

'Sh!' said Dougal.

'How's that?' said Dylan proudly, and Brian measured. 'Thirty feet at least,' swaggered Dylan.

'I make it fifty feet,' said Brian.

'*Fifty*?!' said Dylan. 'It can't be.'

'He's a very good judge,' said Dougal.

'I'm a very good judge,' said Brian.

'He never gets things wrong,' said Dougal.

'I never get things wrong,' said Brian.

'Have another go,' said Brian.

So Dylan prepared to have another go. 'Watch *very* carefully,' he said.

'Oh, we will!' they said, giggling.

'Ready, steady, go,' said Brian.

Dylan leaps again . . .

'Measurement, please,' said Dougal.

And Brian measured . . . 'One foot and a half,' he said.

'Can't be!' said Dylan.

But Brian said it was right.

'I'm never wrong,' he said.

'He's never wrong!' said Dougal.

And Brian said if you had two jumps only the second counted.

'It's the rules,' he said.

'It's the rules,' said Dougal.

And Florence asked if the competition was over and who won.

'I did!' said Dylan.

'I did!' said Dougal.

'He did!' said Brian.

And they all started to talk at once so Florence told them to stop . . .

'Don't all talk at once,' she said.

And Zebedee asked if he could join in the competition. And he did.

'I win!' he said, smiling all round.

And Florence said he was very clever and gave him some flowers and a kiss . . .

'I think you're a professional,' said Dougal.

'No, I'm not,' said Zebedee.

'He's just a good jumper,' said Florence.

'Time for bed then,' said Zebedee.

'Oh, not yet!' said Florence.

'Well you don't want to watch the news, do you?' said Zebedee.

Postman Dougal

Zebedee told Dougal that there was no one to deliver the letters and he was looking for someone intelligent and reliable to be postman.

'Someone . . . er . . . intelligent and reliable?' said Dougal. 'Er . . . someone *particularly* intelligent and *very* reliable?'

'Yes,' said Zebedee. 'Do you know of anyone?'

'Well,' said Dougal. 'Let me see. It's not easy but there is . . . ME!'

'Of course!' said Zebedee. 'Silly of me. I'll just get the letters.'

'Funny he shouldn't have thought of me,' mused Dougal. 'The obvious choice, I would have thought.'

Zebedee brought the letters for Dougal to deliver. 'They'll need sorting out,' he said. 'Good luck.'

And the intelligent and reliable postman was left alone with the letters.

'Let me see now, first things first. Anything for me? Florence, no, Mr Rusty, no, Mr MacHenry, no, Dylan – didn't know he knew anyone who could write. Typical – nothing for the poor, overworked, underpaid postman. Typical . . . Typical!' said Dougal. 'Oh, well, through snow, through hail, through rain, here we go. Lucky the sun's shining.'

Florence told Zebedee that she had sent Dougal a parcel – by post.

'I hope he gets it,' she said.

'Oh dear,' said Zebedee.

'What?' said Florence.

So Zebedee told Florence about Dougal being the postman.

'Oh dear,' said Florence.

'Do you think he's found his parcel?' said Zebedee.

'Do you think he's delivered the letters?' said Florence.

'Time will tell,' said Zebedee. And he said that perhaps Florence should go and see what was happening.

'Yes,' said Florence. So she went to see how Dougal was doing as a postman.

Dougal was exhausted. He had delivered all the letters and parcels.

'Oh, my poor feet,' he said. 'Never again . . . Oh . . . oooh . . .'

'Hello, Dougal,' said Florence.

'Oh, hello,' said Dougal, sighing heavily.

'What's the matter?' said Florence.

'I've had an exhausting day!' said Dougal.

'Being a postman?' said Florence.

'Yes,' said Dougal, 'but never again. There was nothing for *me*, of course.'

'But I sent you a parcel,' said Florence.

'Really? There was one addressed . . .' said Dougal, '"my furry friend", England. Could that be it?'

'Yes, that's it!' said Florence.

Dougal finds the parcel.

'I thought there must be some mistake,' said Dougal, loftily. '"My furry friend", indeed . . . *SUGAR*? You shouldn't have. I'm glad it didn't get lost in the post,' said Dougal. 'Ha! Ha! . . .'

But Dylan came along and told them that *someone* had delivered the letters all wrong.

'Must be a new postman,' he said, yawning, 'who can't read.'

'Oh dear,' said Florence.

'Everyone's looking for him,' said Dylan with a yawn. 'All the letters – all wrong. They're very angry.'

'Oh dear,' said Florence.

'Well,' said Dougal, loudly with a nervous laugh, 'I'd . . . er . . . better go. Lot to do, you know . . . hum . . .'

'Don't worry,' hissed Florence. 'Zebedee will put it right.'

'They all write so badly!' whimpered Dougal, and he left with his sugar.

And when Zebedee arrived Florence told him all about it and, of course, he put it all right again, and made sure everyone had their letters.

'I'm sure he did his best,' said Florence.

'I'm sure he did,' said Zebedee. 'Time for bed.'

A Sticky Problem

Florence was in the garden waiting for Zebedee . . . and when he arrived Florence got a bit of a shock.

'Your moustache is coming off,' she said, faintly.

'I know, isn't it awful?' said Zebedee.

But as luck would have it Mr Rusty arrived – with a pot of glue.

'Isn't that lucky?' said Florence.

'Now we can stick your moustache on properly,' she said, and Zebedee was very grateful.

'I'm very grateful,' said Zebedee.

'It's nothing,' said Florence.

But someone else wasn't being quite so lucky. Dylan's guitar had come apart in his hands.

'Like . . . a calamity,' said Dylan. 'A calamity . . .'

Florence asked what was the matter and Dylan told her about the guitar.

'Well, isn't that lucky?' said Florence.

'Lucky?' said Dylan. 'It's a disaster for music.'

But Florence mended the guitar and explained that it was lucky she happened to have some glue with her.

'Incredible!' said Dylan, and he played Florence a grateful tune.

The music woke Dougal up . . .

'It's obvious,' said Dougal, 'that *someone* didn't know I was asleep. Ha! Ha! SILENCE!'
The guitar music stops, abruptly.

'Thank you,' said Dougal.

The guitar restarts . . .

Perhaps they didn't hear me, thought Dougal. I'll be charitable . . . and calm. I must keep calm . . .

Dougal hums.

'I can't stand it! It's more than flesh and dog can bear,' said Dougal. 'I'LL PUT YOU IN A PIE!'
But the music didn't stop, so Dougal decided he'd have to go and do something about it.

Dougal leaves, growling.

'Ha hum! I wonder if I could trouble you to make a little less noise,' said Dougal.
'Don't like music?' said Dylan.
'On the contrary,' said Dougal. 'I love *music*.'
'So why the . . . like . . . agitation, friend,' said Dylan.
'It stops people sleeping,' said Dougal.
But he was wrong . . . Florence was fast asleep. So Dougal decided it was time for sterner measures, since reason seemed to have failed: he glued the back of the guitar.

'We'd better go,' he whispered. 'Hee hee.'
'Yes,' whispered Dylan. 'Carry the guitar, please.'

He puts the guitar on Dougal's back.

'Take it off! Take it off! Take it off! Take-it-off! I only play the flute,' said Dougal.
'It seems to be . . . like . . . stuck,' said Dylan.
'I can't go around like *this*,' said Dougal. 'People will talk.'
'Where am I?' said Florence, waking.
'You may well ask!' said Dougal. And Dylan told Florence about the guitar being stuck – for some reason.
'I wonder why?' mused Florence.
'Don't stand there musing,' said Dougal. '*Do* something: per-lease.'
'I have . . . like . . . a solution,' said Dylan, and he proposed cutting the guitar off with scissors.
'Over my dead body!' said Dougal. 'Cut my crowning glory? Never!'
And he was off.
'The rabbit's gone dotty! I'd look like a poodle! A *French* poodle!' said Dougal.

Dougal rushes to bed.

'What would people *say*?' said Dougal.
Florence and Dylan were wondering how the guitar came to be stuck to Dougal.
'Did you play a joke on him?' said Florence.

'Madame!' said Dylan. 'I am an innocent rabbit . . .'

So Florence decided she would ask Zebedee to explain the mystery.

'No mystery,' said Zebedee. 'He who plays with glue gets stuck. Good-night.'

Dylan's Beans

Florence told Mr Rusty that she felt like going for a quiet walk in the garden.

'I want to be alone,' she said.

'Ah yes – I know how you feel,' said Mr Rusty, sighing heavily.

'You're so understanding,' said Florence.

And Mr Rusty sighed again . . . and left.

And Florence told Zebedee what she was going to do . . . and Zebedee understood too.

'Would you like to come?' said Florence.

'Not if you want to be alone,' said Zebedee. 'Have a good time.'

'Thank you,' said Florence.

Florence hadn't been alone in the garden for long before she found Dylan's guitar, which was making a strange noise.

How strange, thought Florence and she forgot about wanting to be alone and went to find Dylan.

Meanwhile, Dougal is also in the garden, humming contentedly.

'Mirror, mirror on the wall, who is the fairest dog of all?' said Dougal.

He sees the guitar.

'Hello, hello, hello?! The guitar of my rabbit,' said Dougal, laughing.

A strange rattling noise comes from the guitar.

'What, what, what?! Who's in there? Come out at once!' said Dougal, and they did come out . . . Dylan's jumping beans.

'Get back! Get back! You can't frighten me,' said Dougal, but he was wrong.

The beans, quite frighteningly, begin to chase Dougal.

Meanwhile, Florence found Dylan, asleep as usual.

Dylan yawns and wakes up . . .

So Florence told Dylan about his guitar making funny noises.

'I think you should see to it,' said Florence.

And Dylan asked Florence where it was, because he had something precious inside it.

'It's over here,' said Florence.

Dylan seemed a little agitated and he muttered to himself a lot.

'My beans, my beans. My precious, like, beans,' said Dylan.

'Have a listen,' said Florence. 'Hear anything?'

'Nothing, mam,' said Dylan. 'They must be asleep

again.'

'Who are you talking about?' said Florence.

'My beans,' said Dylan, 'my beautiful jumping beans. Like, hello in there!' he said.

'I think they've gone,' said Florence.

'Oh, don't say that, mam,' said Dylan.

'Well, I can't hear them,' said Florence.

And they were making a lot of noise just now . . .

Dylan went quite pale, and he explained to Florence that we would never get another lot of beans quite like them.

'I'd give anything to find them again,' he said, sadly.

'A reward?' said Florence.

'Yes, mam, even a reward,' said Dylan, gulping.

So they went to look for the beans . . .

'You're sure there's a reward?' said Florence.

'Sure, sure, a reward,' said Dylan.

Meanwhile . . .

'I think that's shaken them,' said Dougal, panting.

But he hadn't shaken them off far because Florence found them.

'There's a reward for these,' she said, happily.

'Good morning, Florence,' said Dougal. 'Ahhh!' he screeched.

'What on earth's the matter, Dougal?' said Florence.

'Those monsters have been chasing me all day,' said Dougal.

But Florence took the beans back to Dylan, who was very happy.

'Do I get a reward?' said Florence.

'Reward?' said Dougal. 'Reward? What reward?'

'The reward is yours, mam,' said Dylan. 'A carrot cake.'

'Thank you very much,' said Florence.

Dougal was beside himself with fury. 'If I hadn't tired them out, you wouldn't have caught them,' he said, huffily. 'I think the reward should be shared – at least.'

But Zebedee said it was time for bed anyway.

'I'll give you a piece, Dougal. Good-night,' whispered Florence.

Father Christmas's Sledge

Mr MacHenry was mending a sledge. It was one that belonged to Father Christmas, and he told Zebedee about it.

'Not like Father Christmas to have an accident,' he said. 'I expect he was overloaded.'

And he asked Zebedee to pass him a few tools, which Zebedee did, in his own particular way.

'Got to get it ready,' said Mr MacHenry. 'It's the one he uses, you know.'

'What for?' said Zebedee.

'To deliver the toys at Christmas,' said Mr MacHenry, 'of course.'

'Oh, of course,' said Zebedee. 'Silly of me.'

'If I don't mend it, he'll have to walk,' said Mr MacHenry.

'I'd better tell Florence about this,' said Zebedee.

Florence was talking to Mr Rusty and wondering where Zebedee was . . . *when Zebedee appeared, with a boing*.

And she was very interested when Zebedee told her about Father Christmas's sledge.

'Let's go and see,' she said, and Zebedee agreed that Florence should certainly go and see.

'Father Christmas needs all the help he can get,' he

said.

'Yes, he's got a very difficult job,' said Mr Rusty, knowingly.

So Florence went.

And Mr MacHenry was still working.

'Oh, it's beautiful,' breathed Florence. 'Father Christmas's sledge. Oh!'

'The very one,' said Mr MacHenry.

Dylan brought some paint for Mr MacHenry, and then decided that he'd better try the sledge for comfort.

Dylan yawns as he gets on to the sledge.

'What *happened* to Father Christmas?' said Florence.

'Oh, he was flying around, having a little practice,' said Mr MacHenry, 'and he hit something . . .'

'Never!' said Florence.

'Yes,' said Mr MacHenry. 'All sorts of things flying about up there, you know. You've got to be very careful. The sky's not what it was. No, no, not what it was, I'm afraid.'

'It doesn't look any different,' said Florence, 'to *me*.'

'No, that's the trouble,' said Mr MacHenry. 'That's what makes it difficult for people like Father Christmas. Well, I must go and make sure everything's ready for him.' And he left.

'Dylan!' said Florence. 'If we wait here we may see Father Christmas!'

Dylan yawns.

'He might give us a ride,' said Florence.

Dylan went quite pale.

'A ride?' he said. 'In this? In the sky?'

'Yes,' said Florence, all excitement.

'Not for me, mam,' said Dylan, 'thank you all the same.'

'Why not?' said Florence, and Dylan explained that he got dizzy very easily, and the thought of rushing around the clouds make him feel quite faint. So he left.

'Hear there's been a bit of trouble,' said Dougal.

'It's all right now,' said Florence. 'It was Father Christmas's sledge – but we've mended it.'

She sighed happily. 'Isn't it lovely?' she said.

'Bit chocolate-boxy,' said Dougal.

But Zebedee congratulated Florence and said he thought Father Christmas would be very grateful.

'He's a lovely man,' said Florence with a sigh. 'Goodnight.'

Dylan's Belt

Dylan was sorting a few things out but, as usual, the effort made him feel a little tired.

Dylan yawns, sleepily.

So he went to sleep.

'Been hard at it then?' said Dougal, laughing. 'I wonder what's in that box? No, I musn't look . . . no . . .'

Dougal hums to himself.

'I wonder what he'd do if I banged a drum?' said Dougal.

Brian was looking for Dougal, who had promised to play him a game of bowls.

'Where have *you* been, lightning?' said Dougal. 'Come on, stir yourself. We're playing a game, remember?'

'I've been looking for *you*, old chum' said Brian.

'Excuses, excuses,' said Dougal. 'Come on, *run!*'

'I'm a snail, remember?' said Brian. 'Great hairy thing . . . Soppy old date . . .' he muttered.

'Come along, come along!' said Dougal. 'Less of this heavy snail acting, per-lease.'

And he prepared to play Brian in a game of bowls.

'I don't think I'll be very good at this game,' said Brian. 'Football is more in my line.'

'Football?' said Dougal with a laugh. 'Football! Snails can't play football.'

Dougal's laughing peters out.

'Can they?' said Dougal.

'Snails are underestimated,' said Brian.

'Snails should be under *something*,' said Dougal.

Meanwhile, Zebedee had decided that Dylan was sleeping too much.

So he woke him up.

'Did you hear,' he said, 'that Dougal and Brian were playing bowls?'

'No, I didn't hear that,' said Dylan. 'That's very interesting.'

'And the children are coming to the garden,' said Zebedee.

'Crazy,' said Dylan, yawning.

'And they all expect to see you up and about and doing things,' said Zebedee. 'And running around . . . and behaving like a rabbit.'

'But I'm a rabbit who *sleeps*,' said Dylan. 'I'm not the hopping kind.'

But Zebedee was gone.

There is the sound of snake-charmer's music as a belt comes out of Dylan's box, and leaves . . .

Zebedee told the children that the garden needed a little stirring up – Dylan was always asleep and Dougal and Brian were always arguing.

'Leave it to us,' they said. 'We'll stir them up.'

But Mr Rusty said his stirring up days were over and he wouldn't come, thank you. So the children went to do a little stirring up.

The belt, meanwhile, comes across the bowls players . . .

'Dougal, old friend,' said Brian, laughing. 'We appear to have company. We have been joined by a moving belt.'

'I believe you are right for once, small mollusc,' said Dougal. 'I wonder where it came from?'

'Ask it,' said Brian.

'Belts aren't able to talk,' said Dougal, witheringly, 'are they?'

But before they could find out, the children arrived to stir things up, and they wanted to know what was going on.

'I'd get out if I were you,' said Dougal to the belt.

'Thank you,' said the belt, leaving.

'You're welcome,' said Dougal.

Dylan came in and asked if anyone had seen a belt.

'I need it for my trousers,' he said.

'I'm fed up with holding up your trousers,' said the belt. 'I never have any fun. You're always asleep – I never get out.'

'Come back,' said Dylan, 'and I'll take you for a long walk. I need you, man.'

'Well,' said the belt, 'if you promise not to sleep so much I'll come back.'

And Dylan said he would try.

'I'll give you one more chance,' said the belt, and they left together.

'Things seem to be stirring up already,' said the children.

'Swinging,' said Brian.

'Time for bed,' said Zebedee.

Soap-Suds Custard

Dylan is looking rather unsuccessfully in a cupboard . . .

Dougal had asked Dylan to fetch him some sugar, as he wanted to make a cake for Florence. But Dylan couldn't find it.

He finally finds something sugar-like, and sets off, spilling it as he goes.

Dougal was waiting patiently . . .

Perhaps a cup of tea? thought Dougal, moving to the kitchen. 'Where *is* he! This is the last time I send that rabbit for anything,' said Dougal.

And Zebedee asked what the matter was.

'I sent that rabbit for some sugar,' said Dougal, 'and he's been gone for *days*. I was thinking of having a little party – with *cakes*! I have a recipe for a sugar cake, the taste of which drives people wild,' he said. '*But I need sugar!*'

'Steady, Dougal,' said Zebedee.

'I just wish that if people say they'll do something, they *do* it, that's all,' said Dougal.

'Very reasonable,' said Zebedee.

Dougal starts to move the furniture around.

'There's always so much to do, you see,' said Dougal, mumbling to himself.

'Can I help?' said Zebedee.

'No, thank you,' said Dougal, running about.

So Zebedee went to tell Florence what was going on.

'It's strange,' said Florence, 'but when Dougal gives a party it always seems to mean a lot of work for other people. But it's very good of him all the same.'

'Perhaps you'd better see what you can do,' said Zebedee.

And Florence said she would.

Meanwhile, Dylan came back with the sugar – or what he *thought* was sugar.

'My, you *have* been quick!' said Dougal. 'Where was it – in the West Indies?'

'I did my best, man,' said Dylan.

'Well, where is it?' said Dougal.

He notices the long trail of sugar behind Dylan . . .

'You spilt it, didn't you?' said Dougal, quietly.

'Sorry,' said Dylan, and Dougal looked closely at the trail of sugar.

Funny, he thought, that looks just like soap powder.

And just at that moment Mr MacHenry decided to do some watering . . .

'*This* will be *very funny*,' sniggered Dougal.

And Mr MacHenry got on with watering.

'Everything's very dry,' he said. 'Very dry.'

'Yes, everything's very dry,' said Dougal.

'Dry,' said Dylan.

The trail of soap powder, for soap powder it is, slowly turns to soap suds, and first Dylan, then Dougal, becomes completely immersed in the suds.

'Very dry – everything,' said Mr MacHenry.

'And Mr MacHenry says the garden needs watering,' said Florence.
'Really?' said Zebedee.

Florence and Zebedee decide to investigate, but soon become completely covered by soap suds as well.

Must be washing-day, thought Florence, but where *is* everybody?
And Zebedee decided it was time to see what was going on . . .

. . . and with a bit of magic, the soap suds disappear.

'I was beginning to think we'd never get out of that,' said Dougal.
'Did the garden good, I expect,' said Mr MacHenry.
'I never did make my cakes,' said Dougal, but Zebedee had . . .
'Just time for some soap-suds custard before bed,' said Florence, laughing a lot.

No Parking

In the garden, Dougal had decided that only authorised parking would be allowed . . .

'And they'll have to pay,' said Dougal, laughing.

Dougal shouts into a loudspeaker.

'Parking here . . . Park your car here . . . Parking here . . . Put your money in the slot,' said Dougal.

'And if they don't they'll be towed away,' said Dougal, laughing again.

The sign was very confusing. One side, 'PARKING' – the other, 'NO PARKING'.

'This could be fun,' said Dougal. 'I'm a fiend,' he laughed.

Florence met Mr Rusty, and they said hello to each other.

Zebedee arrived.

'Ready then?' he said.

'As always,' said Florence.

Dougal was waiting for his first victim. It was Dylan.

'I'll bet he stops,' said Dougal.

Dougal shouts into the loudspeaker.

'Park your car here . . . Parking . . . Parking . . .' said Dougal.

No one can resist a place to park, so Dylan parked. The sign changed.

'No parking,' said Dougal into the loudspeaker. 'You're under arrest.'

Ermintrude was next . . .

'No parking . . . No parking,' said Dougal.

'All right, dear. I heard you,' said Ermintrude.

'You are illegal,' said Dougal.

'I only stopped for a moment,' said Ermintrude.

'That's what they all say,' said Dougal, laughing. 'You're under arrest.'

'I demand to see my lawyer . . .' said Ermintrude, rising into the air, with great determination. 'It's an outrage,' she added (*crashing down to earth again*).

Dougal was enjoying himself immensely . . .

'What does that rabbit think he's doing?' said Dougal, looking at Dylan.

Dylan fails to stifle a yawn.

'He's up to no good, I can tell. He's up to no good,' said Dougal.

The sign turned.

'Park here . . . you may park here,' said the loudspeaker to Brian.

'PLEASE park here,' said the speaker.

'What a *nice* notice,' said Brian.

Dougal laughs.

'Parking?' he asked.

'Don't think so,' said Brian, leaving.

Florence arrived, in a very elegant limousine. She paid her parking fee – two lumps of sugar.

'Are you parked, Dylan?' asked Florence.

Dylan wakes.

'What? What man? Oh . . . this is comfortable . . . I'll take this,' said Dylan.

'You can't do that! Put that sign back at once, you *rabbit*, you! Is nothing sacred? Really!' said Dougal.

'You're very naughty, Dougal,' said Florence, 'but I did put some sugar in the box.'

'What! Put it down . . . put that down!' said Dougal.

'What, man?' said Dylan.

Dylan yawns and goes to sleep.

'You know . . . I think that rabbit could sleep on the M1,' said Dougal.

Dylan's Dream

Dylan was sleeping – a bit restlessly – and dreaming of carrots and other delights, when Dougal came along.

If there was a sleeping contest, thought Dougal, this rabbit would win.

'Better get up,' said Dylan, yawning.

'What we need in this garden is a rabbit-chasing dog – I'm too kind-hearted,' said Dougal.

'Er . . . friend,' said Dylan.

'Yes?' said Dougal.

'Is it daylight yet?' said Dylan.

'Is it *what*?' said Dougal.

'Daylight,' said Dylan. 'Everything seems to be dark. Are you sure it's not still, like, the middle of the night?'

'I'm absolutely positive,' said Dougal. 'I've been up for *hours*.'

Dylan thought about this . . .

'Then there must be some explanation,' he said.

'Try opening your eyes,' said Dougal.

Florence . . . *boing!* . . . met Zebedee.

'Lovely day,' she said.

'You are a comfort,' said Zebedee.

'I know,' said Florence.

Dougal was pondering the problem of Dylan.

'Perhaps I could get him drummed out of the rabbits'

union. For idleness and non-devotion to duty. I don't think I've seen him leaping about and nibbling grass,' said Dougal.

'Hello, Dougal,' said Florence.

Dylan still had his problem. 'If it's dark,' he reasoned, 'it must be night and if it's night I should be sleeping. . .'

'Made any progress?' Dougal asked, as he showed the problem to Florence.

'Don't speak, man,' said Dylan. 'At this time of night you shouldn't be here.'

Brian came along to complicate matters . . .

'Before we get embroiled in snails,' said Dougal, 'may I suggest you lift your ears and let in the light.'

'It's a great idea, man,' said Dylan, 'but they appear to be, like, stuck in this position.'

Brian had brought a boat.

'That's a great help,' said Dougal.

'I'm going boating,' said Brian.

'No, you're not,' said Dougal. 'You are staying here and helping us.'

'Anything you say, old martinet,' said Brian. 'Hello, rabbit.'

'This isn't getting us anywhere,' said Florence. 'We must unstick Dylan's ears.'

'Why?' said Dougal and Brian.

'At least he's quiet like that,' said Dougal.

Dylan was saddened by their lack of sympathy. 'I give you music, friends,' he said, 'will you not give me help?'

'What a heart-rending speech,' said Dougal.

'I'm rent,' said Brian.

'Yes, you would be,' said Dougal. 'I have never known anyone as gullible as you.'

'I'm not gullible – I'm a snail,' said Brian.

But suddenly there was a dramatic change in the situation – Dylan's ears unstuck.

'Daylight,' he said. 'Oh, comfort and joy . . . like . . . joy.'

'Perhaps,' said Dougal, 'we can now get on with life.'

'Yes,' said Dylan, 'I shall sing you a song of life and light.'

Dylan snores.

'Oh, Dylan!' said Florence.

'Oh, mam!' said Dylan.

'Let sleeping rabbits lie,' said Dougal.

'I'm off,' said Brian.

But Florence and Dougal noticed that Brian's boat came adrift from Brian's trailer.

'Oh, a life on the ocean wave,' said Dylan.

'Let's leave,' said Dougal.

Dylan was ecstatic. 'I never realised before,' he said, 'the pleasures of messing about in boats. It makes bed seem somehow tame and adds a new dimension to sleep.'

The Rainbow

Florence called Zebedee, who was hiding . . .

'I was hiding,' he said.

'Yes, I noticed,' said Florence. 'You hide very well.'

'Well, that's my light at a peep,' said Zebedee, 'as they say in Scotland.'

'Shall we go?' said Florence.

In the garden, Dougal had something to show her.

'Take a look at this,' he said.

'This?' said Florence.

'Don't hit it,' said Dougal. 'It's a precision instrument.'

'Oh, a rainbow,' said Florence.

And it was.

'There's just one thing,' said Dougal. 'How many colours?'

Florence counted. 'One, two, three, four, five, six. Six,' she said.

'Exactly,' said Dougal. 'It's wrong. Should be seven. *Someone* has been tampering.'

'Which colour is missing?' said Florence.

'Green,' said Dougal. 'Imagine, a rainbow without green . . .'

Dougal was right – the green was missing.

'What shall we do?' said Florence. 'It's a problem.'

'Got a bit of green about you?' said Dougal.

But Florence said she hadn't.

'Seems a pity people can't leave things alone,' said Dougal. 'Of course, I have my *suspicions*.'

Mr MacHenry came along to have a look at the rainbow, and when they told him the green was missing he had another look – and was forced to agree.

'Do you think he took it?' hissed Dougal. 'He uses a *lot* of green.'

'Mustn't linger,' said Mr MacHenry, to Florence.

'Ask him,' said Dougal.

'Er . . . Mr MacHenry,' said Florence.

'Yes?' said Mr MacHenry.

'Ask him quickly,' said Dougal. 'Trap him.'

'*You* ask him,' said Florence.

'What are you whispering about?' said Mr MacHenry.

'Nothing,' said Dougal, 'except GREEN!!'

'I deny it, I deny it!' said Mr MacHenry.

And he left very fast, denying it . . .

'Methinks the gardener doth protest too much,' said Dougal.

'You have a lovely turn of phrase, Dougal,' said Florence.

'I know,' said Dougal, and they both left.

They found Dylan with a strange machine . . .

'What is it?' said Florence.

'Rainbow painter, mam,' said Dylan.

'Rainbow painter?!' said Dougal.

'Paints rainbows,' said Dylan. 'Works like this . . .'

The machine makes some rather strange noises.

'Does the Met Office know about this?' said Dougal.

Dylan pushes a button.

'One rainbow!' said Dylan.

The machine makes a big sloshing noise and paints a black rainbow.

'Oh my!' said Dylan.
'Very effective,' said Dougal.
Dylan looked, played a little tune in praise of the night he had created, and decided to go to sleep.
'Like, good-night,' he said.
'Well, yes,' said Florence, 'better go to bed, I suppose . . . Good-night.'
'Isn't it *marvellous*?' said Dougal. 'Black everything out without so much as a by-your-leave and then go to bed. I've heard of double British summer time but this is madness, madness.'

Mushroom

Florence said hello to Mr Rusty.

'And hello to you,' said Mr Rusty.

'Seen Zebedee?' said Florence just as Zebedee arrived . . .

'I trust I find you well?' said Zebedee.

'Why shouldn't we be?' said Florence.

Dougal was waiting . . .

'Hello,' said Florence.

Noise.

Mr MacHenry arrived, very excited about something.

Noise.

'Hello,' said Florence.

'I've seen mushrooms growing in the garden,' said Mr MacHenry. 'Two, I've seen – marvellous.'

'How lovely,' said Florence.

'I'm going to look for some more,' said Mr Mac-Henry, and he left to look for some more.

'And so shall we,' said Florence.

'*We*?!' said Dougal. 'If you think I'm picking mushrooms at my time of life, you're off your head.'

Florence took no notice . . .

'I'll trouble you to take notice,' said Dougal. 'And anyway there aren't any mushrooms. Not a single mush!'

'You may be right,' said Florence. 'Come on.'

'And anyway,' said Dougal, following Florence, 'a mushroom hunt is a dodgy business. Say we find *toadstools* in our innocence. The dreaded Death-Cup, for instance, or the False Blusher, hmm?'

'You do go on, Dougal,' said Florence, still searching.

'I wonder where they are?' she mused. 'Only flowers here.'

'You won't be told, will you?' said Dougal, testily.

'No, I won't,' said Florence.

They came across something which looked like a mushroom, but it was only Dylan . . .

'Greetings, mortals,' he said. 'See what I have here? Mushrooms – a great delicacy.'

Dylan goes to sleep and snores.

'I have to admit that rabbit's right,' said Dougal, 'fungus abounds.'

'I would prefer you not to pick *mine*,' said Dylan, waking.

'Oh, no, we *wouldn't*,' said Dougal.

'Finders is, like, keepers,' said Dylan.

'You'll be lucky,' said Dougal.

'What did he say?' said Florence.

'Nothing,' said Dougal.

Dougal slurps.

'I'll just pick *one*,' said Florence.
Florence picks a mushroom and the mushroom grows.

'Gracious! Look at this,' said Florence.
'I'd rather not,' said Dougal. 'I think you've disturbed the balance of nature.'
Florence was intrigued. She picked another . . . and that got bigger too.
'I think you are toying with forces you don't understand,' said Dougal.
'They're magic,' said Florence, prophetically, and she poured some water over it.
'Well,' said Dougal, 'that wouldn't be much good on toast, would it?'

The mushroom changes into a parasol.

'EEK!!' said Dougal.
'Magic,' breathed Florence.
'It's against nature,' said Dougal. 'Someone has been *tampering* . . .'

Florence looks at the parasol, which grows, surprisingly.

The tampering continued.
'I wash my paws of the whole affair,' said Dougal.
But Florence was delighted.

Dylan, in his own way, was guarding his mushroom.

Dylan yawns and slurps.

'Look, Dylan,' said Florence.
Now they'll coo over that for hours, I suppose, thought Dougal and left.

Florence gave the parasol to Dylan, as a present.

'Thank you, mam,' said Dylan.
'You're welcome,' said Florence.
'Just what I needed, mam,' said Dylan, and he fell asleep under it.
Zebedee arrived. 'All happy here?' he asked.
'We've been picking a few mushrooms,' said Florence.
'Sounds a bit dull,' said Zebedee.
'About as dull as a forest fire,' said Dougal, 'what with one thing and another.'
And they left – thereby missing certain happenings . . .

Flower of the Sun

Florence was reading . . .

Dougal coughs. Then he coughs again.

'Got a cold, Dougal?' said Florence.
'No,' said Dougal.
'Oh,' said Florence.
'Reading, are you?' said Dougal.
'Yes, I'm reading about flowers that grow on Mars. It says *here* there's flowers *there*.'
'I would very much doubt that from what I've heard,' said Dougal.
'See for yourself,' said Florence.

Florence throws the book in Dougal's direction.

'Well, there's no need to throw it,' said Dougal. 'Hoity-toity!'

He begins to read.

'Let me see . . . Fresh evidence shows that there may be flowers on the planet Mars. What a pity it may never be proved. Never be proved? Great oafs!' said Dougal.

'What do you mean, Dougal?' said Florence.

'Nothing,' said Dougal, airily.

'No one can go to Mars,' said Florence.

'That's where you're wrong, smarty-breeks,' said Dougal. '*I* intend to go.'

He went to see Mr MacHenry.

'Can I help you?' said Mr MacHenry.

'Just clean out a flower-pot or two, I shall be back soon with some plants from Mars,' said Dougal.

'Your mother's?' said Mr MacHenry.

'The *planet* Mars,' said Dougal, coldly.

'Oh, the *planet* Mars,' said Mr MacHenry.

'Don't wait up,' said Dougal.

'What an extraordinary dog,' said Mr MacHenry.

'A-OK,' said Dougal.

Dougal's rocket takes off.

'Warm here . . . too warm,' said Dylan, yawning.

Aboard the rocket, all was going as well as could be expected.

Florence asked Dylan if he'd seen the launch and Dylan said he hadn't.

'Really!' said Florence.

'I was not informed, mam,' said Dylan, yawning.

Florence was worried . . .

'Don't worry, mam,' said Dylan, 'that dog is indestructible . . .'

The indestructible dog had arrived on Mars.

'Now what have I come for? Oh yes, Mars flowers. The

things I do in the cause of science,' said Dougal. 'I claim the planet for Queen Elizabeth the second – lovely lady.'

'Now . . . better have a look round, I suppose,' said Dougal.

Dougal looks through the window and the door and then gets out.

'If there are any flowers here, I'm a snail,' said Dougal. 'Still, better be intrepid, I suppose – it is expected of one.'

Dougal intrepidly starts to explore.

'Anyone about?' said Dougal.

Dougal had a good look about for the Mars flower, but he couldn't see it anywhere. In fact, he couldn't see anything.

'Funny place! Better use my patent plant-detector, I suppose,' said Dougal.

Dougal starts to hum, and puts the plant-detector down.

'Right, detect something, you,' said Dougal.

The detector detects something, and beeps.

'Well, I'm not staying here much longer, flowers or no flowers. What's that rumbling . . . ?' said Dougal.

There is a screech and a bag appears.

'A native. I shall capture him or her,' said Dougal.
So Dougal set off back with his capture.
Meanwhile, back on Earth, Florence was waiting.
'Look, man,' said Dylan.

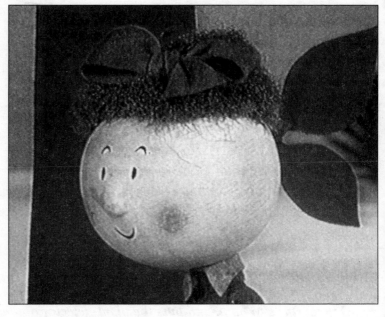

There is a tremendous noise as the rocket arrives and lands.

'Are you all right, Dougal?' said Florence.
'A pinpoint landing, I see,' said Dougal.
'Any flowers?' said Florence.
'Typical!' said Dougal. 'I fly 34,000,000 miles and not even one cup of tea when I get back.'
'Nothing then?' said Florence.

'I've got a small native,' said Dougal.

'It looks like the sandwich bag you took with you,' said Florence.

'Ask for its passport,' said Dougal.

Florence's Party

Florence arrived at the Roundabout . . .

'Something special about today,' said Mr Rusty, 'and I can't think what it is.'

'It's my birthday for one thing,' said Florence, 'and I got some hankies.'

'Your birthday!' said Mr Rusty. 'We must do something.'

Zebedee arrived . . .

'My birthday,' said Florence.

'Really?!' said Zebedee.

'We must *do* something,' said Mr Rusty, and Zebedee agreed.

'Something very extra special,' said Zebedee.

In the garden, Mr Rusty seemed to know something that Florence didn't.

'What's happening?' she asked Brian.

'Nothing,' said Brian.

Florence couldn't understand it . . .

'What's happening?' she asked Ermintrude.

'Nothing, dear heart,' said Ermintrude. 'Nothing at all.'

Florence was more puzzled than ever . . .

Something's going on, she thought.

'What's happening?' she asked Dougal.

'Nothing,' said Dougal. 'Nothing at all. Absolutely
nothing at all . . . *Nothing*.'

Florence nearly cried . . .

'What's happening?' she asked Dylan.

'Like . . . nothing, mam,' said Dylan.

Florence tried not to care . . .

'Coming over?' said Mr Rusty.

'Where?' said Florence, sadly.

'Over here,' said Mr Rusty.

So Florence went and found a birthday surprise.

'Special birthday show,' said Mr Rusty, 'for our very
talented and beautiful friend . . . er . . . what's her name
now . . . er . . .'

'Florence,' said Florence.

'Florence, of course,' said Mr Rusty. 'And first we have "THE GREAT DYLAN".'

Dylan juggled beautifully and gave Florence a present.

'Oh, thank you,' said Florence.

'You're welcome, mam,' said Dylan.

'Next we have "THE GREAT MACHENRY",' said Mr Rusty.

Mr MacHenry did great things with a hat and some flowers and then presented the bouquet to Florence.

'Next we have "THE GREAT . . . THE GREAT . . .er . . . oh yes. THE GREAT ZEBEDEE",' said Mr Rusty.

Zebedee did some great things and then presented Florence with a special birthday book.

'I hope you have a very happy day,' he said.

'Thank you,' said Florence.

'And now,' said Mr Rusty, '"THE GREAT DOUGAL".'

'Ha! Hum!' said Dougal.

Dougal performs his little-seen high-wire act.

'Something for you. A little token . . . of my esteem,' said Dougal, with a little cough. There was a skipping rope – and a parcel.

'Happy birthday,' said Dougal.

'Thank you,' said Florence.

'And now,' said Mr Rusty, '"THE GREAT ERMINTRUDE AND BRIAN".'

Brian with a hoop: Ermintrude runs towards the

hoop and crashes.

'Whoops!' said Brian. 'Happy birthday.'
'Me too!!' said Ermintrude.
'She's past it, poor old thing,' said Brian.
Florence thanked them for their birthday tricks and gathered up all her presents.
'Had a good day?' said Mr Rusty.
'Yes, thank you,' said Florence, crying.
'Keep your voice from weeping and your eyes from tears,' said Dougal, unexpectedly.

Captured Storm

Mr Rusty was dreaming . . .

'Oh . . . Oh dear . . . Oh dear,' said Mr Rusty.

He wakes up, to find that Florence has come to visit him, surprisingly.

'Dreamed you weren't coming to see me any more,' he told Florence.

'What a terrible dream,' said Florence.

Zebedee arrived. 'Trouble in the garden,' he said.

'That'll make a change,' said Florence.

'Oh, Miss Sharp today, aren't we?' said Zebedee.

'I don't know what you mean,' said Florence.

Dougal was waiting . . . cowering a little.

'Why are you cowering, Dougal?' said Florence.

'Who's cowering? I'm not cowering. Why should I cower?' said Dougal.

Dylan was cowering too – in his own fashion.

'Oh, my head,' he said. 'The . . . like . . . heaviness.'

Ermintrude wasn't exactly cowering because she didn't think it was dignified, but she *was* perturbed about *something*.

And so was Brian. 'I have a feeling something's about to *happen*,' he said.

'What's the matter with you all?' said Florence.

'My head hurts, mam,' said Dylan.

'Oh,' said Florence.

'I'm *worried*,' said Ermintrude.

'Oh,' said Florence.

'*I'm* worried,' said Brian.

'You're worrying,' said Dougal. 'I expect it's all your fault.'

'It's not my fault,' said Brian.

Brian walks past Dougal.

'Great hairy lump!' said Brian, in a low voice.

Mr MacHenry came along. 'Bottle for you,' he said.

Florence was mystified. 'What *is* going on?' she asked.

'Well, something's going to happen,' said Mr MacHenry, 'so I thought I'd bring you a bottle – just in case.'

'In case of *what*?' said Florence.

'You may well ask,' said Dougal.

'Dougal, this has got to stop,' said Florence.

'Stop? It's just starting,' said Dougal.

Storm noises come from the bottle.

'Gracious,' said Florence.

There is a boing as Zebedee enters.

'It's a thunderbolt – in the bottle . . . Do something,'

said Florence.

Zebedee did something – fast.

Zebedee bravely sits on the bottle.

'Goodness, you're brave,' said Florence.

'No good will come of this,' said Dougal. 'What happens when you get off, answer me that!'

'I hadn't thought,' said Zebedee.

'Better start then,' said Dougal.

'Should we go?' said Florence.

'If you want to abandon me in my hour of need, yes,' said Zebedee.

The noise reaches a crescendo, accompanied by fireworks.

'He's in orbit,' said Florence.

They look up to see that a rainbow has formed.

And Zebedee has certainly saved the day . . .

'Time for bed then,' said Zebedee.

'Yes, I think I'm ready for my bed,' said Florence.

'Bed? Bed? I'll never sleep again. How do you expect me to sleep with thunderballs flying under the bed? I'm not made of stone, you know. I'm sensitive,' said Dougal.

Dylan, Hairdresser

Brian was waiting for Dougal, who seemed to be in a hurry.

'Oh, I got up so late this morning I don't know whether I'm coming or going,' said Dougal.

'You're *going*, old speedy mate,' said Brian.

'I've got a million things to do and I've not had time to put a comb through my hair yet . . .'

'Looks like it,' said Brian. 'Bit shaggier than usual, if that's possible.'

'What?!' said Dougal. 'Choose your words, snail.'

'It's true – you could do with having your barnet trimmed.'

'What a vulgar expression,' said Dougal.

'I'm a vulgar snail,' said Brian.

'You can say that again,' said Dougal.

'Get your hair cut,' said Brian.

'I will,' said Dougal, 'if I can find someone sufficiently . . . sensitive. Someone who realises that I don't just want a quick top and tail. In short . . . in short . . . an artiste.'

Florence met Mr Rusty and they passed the time of day.

'Lovely day,' said Florence.

'Beautiful,' said Mr Rusty. 'Like you . . .'

'Thank you,' said Florence.

Zebedee arrived.

'Late as usual,' said Florence.

'You'll make me cry,' said Zebedee.

'No, I won't,' said Florence.

She looked for Dougal and couldn't see him anywhere.

'I wonder where he is,' she mused.

She saw *something*. 'Never seen that before. I wonder what it is?' said Florence.

There was a noise. Florence stopped and was amazed to see Dylan apparently working.

'Why, Dylan!' said Florence.

'Mam . . . welcome. Welcome to my hairdressing boutique . . . like . . . welcome.'

'Are you . . . like . . . comfortable, sir?' said Dylan.

'Sir' was Dougal.

'Don't disturb the curlers, sir, until I use the setting lotion,' said Dylan.

'Curlers?' said Florence, aghast. 'Setting lotion?!'

'Sir, you really must keep still or all my efforts are ruined,' said Dylan.

Dylan looks in the mirror.

'Ruined! Ruined! Ruined, like . . . er . . . ruined! Er . . . pardon me,' said Dylan.

Florence had never seen Dylan like this – he seemed quite agitated and distraught.

'Er . . . perhaps you'd care to look, sir,' said Dylan.

'Sir' looked.

'Can't see anything,' said Dougal.

'One needs to remove the towel,' said Dylan. 'If you'll just wait a moment I'll take it off!'

'Don't you dare!' said Dougal.

Florence pretended not to know who it was and said 'hello' very politely.

'Helloo!' said Dougal.

And Florence waited for something to happen and something happened all right . . .

Dylan removes the towel and runs.

'Where are you going?' asked Dougal. 'You haven't finished yet, you rabbit you!'

Florence found herself losing control . . .

'How do I look?' said Dougal. '*Chic*? *Elegante*? That's what I was promised.'

'Have a look,' said Florence.

So Dougal looked . . .

'What's that sheep doing there,' said Dougal, laughing. 'It's me! It's me!! I'll sue him . . . I'll bury his guitar . . . I'll . . . Aahh!!' said Dougal. 'You wait till I find him. I'll make him rue the day he set foot in this garden . . . savage! Call yourself a hairdresser . . . you . . . couldn't hairdress a football. Come back . . .'

Happy Birthday, Dylan

Florence arrived at the Roundabout. It was Dylan's birthday. She'd brought him a present and was just wondering if anyone else would have remembered to bring one when Mr Rusty arrived – carrying a parcel.

'Sorry to be late,' he said, 'I was getting this present.'

'Oh, I'm glad you remembered,' said Florence.

'Remembered what?' said Zebedee. 'Dylan's birthday by any chance? I've got him a little something somewhere . . . Ah, there it is.'

'He's going to have a lot of presents,' said Florence. 'I think we should go . . .'

In the garden, Dougal had his present all wrapped up.

'Er . . . what have *you* got him?' he asked. 'Something nice?'

'I'm not telling you,' said Florence.

'Oh go on . . . don't be rotten,' said Dougal. 'Go on, tell me.'

'No,' said Florence.

'Is it a bicycle?' said Dougal.

'No,' said Florence.

'Er . . . plastic model of a lettuce?' said Dougal.

'No,' said Florence.

'Er . . . A guitar with a three speed?' said Dougal.

'No,' said Florence. 'You'll never guess, Dougal.'

Dylan's presents were arriving thick and fast . . .

'Er . . . would you care to tell me what you've bought?' said Dougal.

'Certainly not, it's a deadly secret,' said Brian.

'Deadly,' said Ermintrude.

'Rotten lot,' said Dougal.

Mr MacHenry brought *his* present, and Mr Rusty said he thought they'd better go and give them to Dylan before he got any older.

'Asleep,' said Mr MacHenry.

'Now, all together,' said Brian.

'Happy Birthday, Dylan,' they said, all together.

Dylan was overcome.

'I am overcome . . . like . . . overwhelmed,' he said. 'Like . . . *shattered* even . . . even.'

'Well there's no need to be shattered,' said Dougal. 'It's only a few presents, it's not National Rabbit Week.'

'Oh it's . . . like . . . too much,' said Dylan.

And he opened the first present . . . a tie.

'Just what I wanted,' he said.

'That's mine,' said Brian. 'I bought him that with my impeccable good taste.'

'I wish you'd told me,' said Florence.

'Told you what?' said Brian.

It became obvious – Florence had bought a tie too.

'Er . . . just what I wanted, mam,' said Dylan.

'Oh dear,' said Dougal.

The ties continued to appear . . .

'What can I say?' said Dylan.

'Perhaps you could knit them into a mat,' said Ermintrude.

'Oh no, they're beautiful – beautiful,' said Dylan.

'Just rather a lot of them,' said Mr MacHenry.

'Well, I won't have to buy another tie for . . . for . . . weeks,' said Dylan.

'That's the truth,' said Mr Rusty, who'd brought a tie too.

'I would just like to say thank you to *everyone*,' said Dylan.

'I think that's sweet, *considering*,' said Ermintrude.

Zebedee arrived with his parcel.

'If it's a tie, I wouldn't bother,' said Brian with a

laugh.

'No, it's not a tie,' said Zebedee.

'Open it!' they said.

Dylan did so . . . 'Er . . . crazy, man,' he said. 'What is it?'

'Isn't it obvious?' said Zebedee. 'It's a special box to keep ties in. It holds 453.'

'You wait,' said Dougal.

A Starry Night

Dougal and Florence were up rather late one day, and wondering where all the stars had gone . . .

'Do you think it's cloudy?' said Florence.

'That would be the simple explanation,' said Dougal.

'What do you mean?' said Florence.

'Well, you never know in this place, do you? I expect someone's switched them off,' said Dougal.

'Oh, can you do that?' said Florence.

'Can you do it? Of course you can do it!' said Dougal.

'Oh, I didn't know,' said Florence.

'The ignorance!' said Dougal.

'I didn't come here to be insulted,' said Florence.

'Oh, hoity-toity!' said Dougal.

'And anyway I'm not at all sure you're right,' said Florence.

'Have you ever known me to be wrong?' said Dougal.

Florence looked at him.

'Well, about basic well-known things like stars, I mean,' said Dougal. 'I . . . er . . . may have made little errors in the past about minor matters . . . er . . . I'm only human, you know.'

'But you're *not* human,' said Florence.

'Well, if you're going to get personal,' said Dougal, 'you can go and look at the stars with someone else. *I* won't care.'

And he got all huffy.

'No need to get all huffy!' said Florence.

'Who's huffy?' said Dougal. 'I'm never huffy!'

'I only said you weren't human,' said Florence. 'And you get huffy.'

'I thought we came to look at the stars,' said Dougal, huffily.

So they counted the stars, which had come out during the argument, and found there were still quite a lot missing.

'Quite a lot missing,' said Dougal, darkly. 'Someone has been *tampering*.'

So they counted them again.

'I make it one short now,' said Dougal.

'I wonder where it is?' said Florence.

Dylan arrived . . .

'I found the craziest thing over there,' he said.

'Over where?' said Dougal. 'Over where?'

'Why, over there, man,' said Dylan. 'Craziest thing you ever saw.'

'I presume eventually he'll tell me what it is,' said Dougal.

But Dylan said he'd *show* them what it was.

And it was the missing star – come down into the garden for a change of scene.

'It's a bit dark here, isn't it?' said the Star sweetly.

'Well, what do you expect?' said Dougal. 'You're supposed to be up there shining away. On strike, I suppose.'

'It's very pretty,' said Florence.

'Thank you,' said the Star. 'You may call me Estelle.'

'Estelle?' said Florence.

'Well, it should be Stella, but I changed it because I think Estelle is much more suitable these days, don't you? Any star who is anyone is called Estelle,' said the Star.

'I don't know what this garden's coming to,' said Dougal. 'I really don't.'

'Oh, you!' said Florence.

Dylan plays the guitar.

'Oh, I feel like lighting up,' said the Star.

'Back to work, I hope,' said Dougal.

'I wish I was a star,' said Florence, sighing.

Dylan and the Guitar

Dylan woke up full of energy . . .

Exercise is the greatest thing, he thought, in moderation.

'You're at it again, aren't you?' said Dougal.

And Dylan was . . .

'Wake up!' said Dougal. 'Don't you ever get tired doing all that sleeping?'

'I've not given it a lot of thought, man,' said Dylan.

'Well, it's about time you *did*,' said Dougal. 'You'll grow roots?'

'Promise?' said Dylan.

Zebedee arrived and had a look around. 'Anything happening?' he asked.

'Only in the most negative sense,' said Dougal.

'Anything happening?' said Florence.

'Only if you are interested in negative events,' said Zebedee.

'Oh,' said Florence.

Dylan continues to snore, energetically.

'The phantom snorer strikes again,' said Dougal.

'Wake him up,' said Florence.

'That would require an Act of Parliament,' said

Dougal.

'Greetings, friends,' said Dylan. 'I have decided to take more exercise in future. The trouble is I keep falling asleep before I can start.'

'You absolutely amaze us,' they said.

'Luckily,' said Dylan, 'when I'm asleep I dream I'm playing . . . it's exhausting.'

And Dylan dreamed he was playing again – although sometimes the guitar seemed to be playing him.

Dylan woke up, exhausted.

'You've been asleep,' said Florence.

'I know, mam. I'm not sure I can keep it up. I'll lose *pounds*,' said Dylan yawning.

Zebedee arrived. 'Everyone fit?' he said. 'Because it's time to race off to bed.'

The Exhibition

Florence was waiting for Zebedee . . . who arrived.

'I'm a bit late,' he said, 'because I was trying to get a ticket for the exhibition.'

'What exhibition?' said Florence.

'The one in the garden,' said Zebedee. 'The one everyone has been talking about. It's very difficult to get a ticket, so I shouldn't bother to go if I were you. You won't be able to get in and then you'll be disappointed.'

'Oh, you are *infuriating*,' said Florence. 'Of course I shall get in.'

Dougal, and the others, were waiting.

'Hello,' said Florence, brightly.

'Got your ticket?' said Dougal, laughing. 'Very difficult to get in without a ticket, you know . . . Got a ticket?'

'Oh, *Dougal*!' said Florence.

Dylan told Florence she didn't have to have a ticket.

'Do *I* have to have a ticket?' said Ermintrude.

'No, mam,' said Dylan. 'Anyone with a tail gets in free. So you qualify.' He laughed.

'When you're all *quite* finished,' said Dougal.

'Lead on, mighty leader,' said Brian.

And they all went to the exhibition which Florence had been asked to open.

'I declare this exhibition open,' she said.
'Very prettily done,' said Dougal.
It was an exhibition of pictures.

'How *lovely*,' said Florence.

Dougal looks at a portrait. Of Brian.

'Not quite the word I would have chosen,' said Dougal, laughing. 'Annigonioni's latest, I presume?'

Brian looks at a picture of a carrot.

Brian found a picture he liked.

'What delicate brushwork,' he said. 'That'll look good in my kitchen.'

Ermintrude looks at the Mona Lisa.

'This one seems familiar,' said Ermintrude. 'Is it you, Florence dear?'

They looked at Brian's portrait.

'A very good likeness,' said Ermintrude.

'Has it caught the essential *me?*' said Brian.

'Nothing's essential about you,' said Dougal.

'Don't be unkind,' said Ermintrude.

They looked around some more. Brian and Dylan admired the carrot picture as connoisseurs.

'Four carrots in a fog,' said Dougal, laughing.

'Look over here,' said Ermintrude.

'My effort, mam,' said Dylan, modestly.

'I may sue,' said Ermintrude.

'You wouldn't stand still!' said Dylan.

'I like it! I like it!' said Brian.

'You like anything,' said Dougal.

'Well, I think they're all lovely,' said Ermintrude. 'Don't you?'

'Yes, they said, even though Dougal had some doubts about Brian's portrait – and said so.

And they all had doubts about another portrait. For some reason it seemed a little familiar – although they couldn't place the face.

'What *I* want to know,' said Dougal, 'is what she's laughing at.'

'She's smiling,' said Florence.

'Well I think she's got a very funny look on her face,' said Dougal. 'And I wouldn't want to meet her in the garden after dark. I can tell you *that*.'

'Come to think of it I wouldn't want to meet anything in the garden after dark,' said Dougal.

The Moody Concerto

Florence called to Zebedee.

'You called, madam, and I arrive,' he said. 'Your wish is my command, as they say.' And he did a little twirl.

'I'm in good twirling form today,' he said. 'Want to do anything special? Trip to the moon? Round the world? Visit the garden?'

'The garden, I think,' said Florence.

'Ah, I think you're wise,' said Zebedee. 'Shall we go?'

And they went.

Florence greeted Dougal.

'Oh, I'm glad you've arrived,' he said. 'I'm having a terrible time today. I can't tell you what it's like here. Listen, if you can bear to, because I can't . . .'

Dylan and Brian are playing music.

'That,' said Dougal, 'has been going on since I got up. I'm thinking of suing someone – if it's only the BBC.'

'But who is it?' asked Florence.

'Who do you think?' said Dougal. 'It's that rabbit and that snail – great clumps. Silence!'

'It seems we are not appreciated, snail friend,' said Dylan.

'I think you're right, maestro,' said Brian.

Dylan tried again, but it wasn't very good.

'Er . . . Dylan,' said Florence.

'Mam,' said Dylan in a raised voice, 'I am trying to interpret this very difficult music and I must ask you not to interrupt . . .ooh.'

'Cheek!' said Dougal.

'He is an *artiste*,' said Brian. 'And so am I.'

'You're about as artistic as a bottle of red cabbage,' said Dougal, 'and not nearly so pretty. Oh, come on, I'll give you a hand.'

Dougal shows them how to do it . . .

Florence could stand it no longer.

'You must have the music upside down,' she said.

Dougal was deeply humiliated. 'I'll never get into the Proms now,' he said, 'and I was looking forward to giving them "Land of Hope and Glory" and a snatch of the 1813.'

'I can't read music, anyway,' said Brian, while Florence turned the music round.

They play again.

'If that's the food of love, I'm not hungry,' said Dougal.

Pancakes

Florence asked Mr Rusty if Zebedee had arrived yet and
Mr Rusty said he hadn't.

'Oh,' said Florence, and Zebedee arrived.

'I hear tales of cooking in the garden,' he said.

'Now, let me see . . . have I got everything? Oh dear,
people come to *plague* me,' said Dougal.

'We haven't come to plague you,' they said.

'We're spectators,' they said.

'Oh joy,' said Dougal, heavily.

'What you making, old cooker?' said Brian.

'Pancakes,' said Dougal.

'You're lovely,' said Brian.

Florence read the recipe . . .

'Has it got lettuce in it?' said Brian.

'Don't think so,' said Florence.

'No lettuce!?' said Brian. 'How rotten!'

'Will someone silence that mollusc?' said Dougal.
'Now, where am I?'

'I don't think you often have lettuce in pancakes, do
you?' said Mr Rusty, reasonably.

'I do,' said Brian, 'invariably. Or cabbage.'

'What next?' said Dougal.

'Milk?' said Florence.

'Well yes, I'm waiting for the milk, aren't I?' said

Dougal.

Ermintrude arrives.

'About time,' said Dougal.
'Herbs?' said Florence.
'I'm waiting for those too,' said Dougal.
The herbs arrived . . .
'Here we are,' said Mr MacHenry. 'Essence of herb –
straight from the garden.'
'Well perhaps I can get on now,' said Dougal.
'Yes, I think you probably can,' said Florence.
And Dylan said he'd play some pancake music to help
things along.

*Dylan plays for a while, then, overcome, he sleeps
and snores.*

Dylan dropped off but the pancake making went on.
Dougal stirred and stirred and Ermintrude added milk,
and Dougal stirred again.
Dylan, refreshed, played on. 'Stir, man, stir!' he said.
Mr MacHenry added essence of herb.
'This can be very tiring,' said Dougal.
'When are we going to . . . like . . . eat, man?' said
Dylan.
'Hmm, I *love* a pancake,' said Ermintrude.
Florence cooked the first pancake.
'Careful!' said Mr Rusty. 'Don't burn yourself. Now
toss the pancake in the air – that's the right way.'

So Florence tossed the pancake.
'Bravo!' said Ermintrude.
'My turn,' said Dougal.
But Dylan got there first . . .

Pancake lands on Brian.

'Suits you, snail,' said Dougal, giggling.
'I'm a failure, man,' said Dylan.
'Yes, you are,' said Brian. 'Hit me right on the bonce.'
'Are you implying my pancakes are heavy?' said Dougal. 'I make the lightest pancakes in the world. In the trade they are known as Dougal's Delights.'

A Picnic

'Er, is this the day we were going to have our picnic?' said Mr Rusty.

'Yes, it is,' said Florence. 'Have you got everything?'

'Er, everything?' said Mr Rusty.

'For the picnic,' said Florence.

'Oh yes, the picnic,' said Mr Rusty and he went away mumbling.

They waited for him.

'I hope you've remembered the corkscrew,' said Zebedee, 'but if that's all you forget it should be a great success. Off you go.'

So they went.

Dougal was ready for the picnic.

'Got everything?' he said. 'Corkscrew? No one ever remembers a corkscrew . . .'

'Well, we've remembered,' said Florence.

'And a tablecloth?' said Dougal. 'I'm not eating off the bare ground, you know. I've got a tablecloth . . . damask . . . none of your plastic.'

'Oh, come *on*,' said Florence.

Mr Rusty wasn't sure they'd remembered everything. 'I feel sure there's *something*,' he said.

'I've remembered the salt and pepper,' said Brian. 'I am the most useful and resourceful of snails, you must admit. All together now, for he's a jolly good fellow!'

'That'll do, Brian,' said Florence.

'Sorry,' said Brian.

'Will here do?' said Florence.

'Any ants?' said Dougal. 'I can't abide an ant.'

'We're not all here yet,' said Mr Rusty, waving the corkscrew.

Ermintrude arrived.

'I love a picnic,' she mooed. 'It's so lovely eating out of doors.'

'What *is* she on about?' said Dougal. 'She always eats out of doors – it's a well known habit of cows, eating out of doors.'

'I'll bet no one's remembered a corkscrew,' said Ermintrude. 'And salt and pepper.'

'Oh, yes we have,' said Mr Rusty and Brian. 'So there!'

Dylan arrived.

'I've brought these cushions for the picnic,' he said, 'because I feel like everyone should be . . . like . . . comfortable, man. Comfort is very important at picnics.'

Mr MacHenry had brought all sorts of useful things like knives and forks and spoons and plates and vases of flowers and place mats . . .

'No finger-bowls?' said Dougal.

Brian and Mr Rusty started to lay the table, helped by Ermintrude and watched by Dylan.

Florence took the cushions.

'Nearly ready?' said Dylan. 'Then I'll arrive.'

'Looks very pretty,' said Brian, and Dougal and

Florence agreed and so did Mr Rusty and Ermintrude.

'*Very* pretty,' they said.

'There's just one thing,' said Dylan, 'Did anyone bring any . . . like . . . food?'

'Food?' said Mr MacHenry.

'I don't think I can bear it,' said Dougal.

And they all realised they had forgotten to bring the food.

'We're all soppy,' said Brian.

'No one can possibly realise how humiliated I feel,' said Dougal.

The Flying Saucer

Mr MacHenry had lost something and was looking for it.

'Wherever can it be?' he said.

Florence came along.

'Hello,' she said.

'You haven't seen it by any chance, have you?' said Mr MacHenry.

'Seen what?' said Florence.

'It's escaped,' said Mr MacHenry. 'It's very worrying . . .'

Dougal was looking for something too. 'Now where is it?' he said.

'Where's what?' said Florence. 'What's everyone looking for?'

'I can't find it anywhere,' said Brian.

'No, you *couldn't*,' said Dougal. 'Typical!'

'Don't be like that!' said Brian.

'What *is* it?' said Florence.

'I don't know,' said Brian. 'I was just told to look for it and I always do as I'm told, because I'm little and loveable and everyone takes advantage of me. Of course I mention no names but watch where my eyes rest . . .' Brian laughs.

'Can't find it, dear heart,' said Ermintrude.

'Well it's big enough,' said Dougal.

'Nevertheless . . .' said Ermintrude.

'Really!' said Dougal.

'It would help if we knew what we were looking for,' said Ermintrude.

'Exactly!' said Brian. 'We need information.'

'Can't find it, man,' said Dylan. 'Like . . . nowhere.'

'I'm not surprised,' said Ermintrude.

Suddenly they heard something.

They all look skywards to try to see where the strange beeping was coming from.

'That's it!' said Dougal.

'What is?' said Brian.

'*That!*' said Dougal. 'Scatter and find it!'

So they scattered to find it.

'I scattered the wrong way,' said Brian.

A strange object appeared.

'That's it,' hissed Dougal.

It landed . . .

'MOO,' said Ermintrude.

'Oooh!' said Brian.

The flying saucer, for such it appears to be, rises and leaves, beeping.

'Well I never,' said Ermintrude. 'Whatever next?'

'That was *it*,' said Dougal.

'If I'd known I'd never have looked,' said

Ermintrude. 'What a fright I got.'

'Was that it?' said Brian.

'Yes, was it?' said Dylan. 'Like . . . er . . . it?'

And they said it was.

'Crazy,' said Dylan.

'I couldn't agree more,' said Ermintrude. 'Horrible thing.'

Mr MacHenry came back and told them he still couldn't find it anywhere.

They asked him what *he* was looking for.

'It's my new flying planting machine,' he said. 'It flies.'

'Does it indeed!' said Dougal.

'Yes, it does,' said Mr MacHenry. 'I call it the flying saucer.'

'That's what I wanted you to find,' said Dougal.

'Well we found it, dear thing,' said Ermintrude.

'Er . . . I don't want to worry anyone,' said Dylan.

'What do you mean?' said Mr MacHenry, worried.

'Well it's that machine of yours,' said Dylan. 'It's like driving me crazy. It keeps planting things and every time I want to take a little sleep it . . . like . . . wakes me up and plants something on me. I got an earful of primrose roots, man. I mean flower power is one thing but this is ridiculous . . . ridiculous.'

'Time for bed, I suppose,' said Florence.

'How do you expect me to sleep,' said Dougal, 'with *that* thing about . . . ?'

Dylan, Sculptor

'How much longer?' said Dougal. 'I've got a crick in my neck, my left front foot's gone to sleep and my nerves are *jangling* . . . jangling.'

'Nearly finished, man,' said Dylan.

'Have you caught the essential me?' said Dougal. For Dylan was making a sculpture of Dougal . . .

'I wouldn't want anyone to see it before it's finished. Do you think that "Do not disturb" notice will keep them away?' said Dougal.

Meanwhile, Florence and Mr Rusty were talking . . .

'What do you think of the International Situation?' said Florence.

'I try not to,' said Mr Rusty.

'Very wise,' said Florence. 'I wonder where Zebedee is?'

And they called him and he arrived.

'There's something *creative* going on in the garden,' he said.

'Oooh!' said Florence.

'Oooh!' said Ermintrude. 'Oooh . . . I can't begin to tell you what's going on here.'

'Try,' said Florence.

'Have one guess,' said Ermintrude. 'Go on.'

'You've jumped over the moon,' said Mr Rusty.

'Silly thing,' said Ermintrude. 'I don't do that any

more.' And she went to see how Dougal's sculpture was coming on.

'Please, mam!' said Dylan. 'It's not finished yet.'

'We'll let you know,' said Dougal.

'It's not finished yet – they're going to let us know,' said Ermintrude. 'Oh, the excitement of it all, tra-la!'

'What?' said Florence.

'Secret,' said Ermintrude.

Dylan carried on working . . .

'Seven inches! Wow!' he said.

'What do you mean, "Wow!"?' said Dougal.

'It's just . . . like . . . I have to rethink the nose, man. It's seven inches across . . . like . . . Wow!' said Dylan. 'That is an epic nose. WOW!'

'It's nothing,' said Dougal.

'Hello! Hello!' said Brian, much to Dylan's fury. He had to have silence while he was working, he said.

'So zip your screamer,' said Dougal, rather coarsely.

'Oh!' said Brian. 'Did you hear that?' (*he added to the expectant group outside.*)

The train arrived. Dylan was in despair . . .

'Anyone want to go anywhere?' said the train.

'I just want silence,' said Dylan, slightly hysterically.

'You've upset him now,' said Dougal.

'Well I don't know, I'm sure,' said the train. 'Open your mouth and you get your funnel bitten off. It wasn't like this in the sidings of Clapham, I can tell you.' And she left.

'I've never seen anything like it in all my puff,' said the train.

Mr MacHenry arrives. Noisily, unfortunately . . .

'Sorry,' said Mr MacHenry.

And Dylan said he really didn't know what he was doing any more.

'Doesn't look like it,' said Dougal.

'Hello all!' said Mr MacHenry, as he sees the others.

Dylan lost control . . .

'He's lost control,' said Dougal.

'Who's not to be disturbed?' said Mr Rusty.

'I can't go on!' said Dylan. 'I can't.'

Something went on . . .

'I've got something to say,' said the clay statue. 'It's, like, time for bed, babies.'

The Orchestra

Zebedee had gathered together an orchestra and the concert was about to begin . . .

'Follow me closely,' he said, hopefully.

And they all said they would.

Zebedee taps while Florence, Dylan, Dougal, Brian and Ermintrude begin to play.

Ermintrude was worried . . .

'Am I doing it right, darlings?' said Ermintrude.

'No, you're jolly well not!' said Brian.

'I thought not,' said Ermintrude.

'May we try again?' said Zebedee.

Ermintrude's hoof opens the lid of the piano she's playing.

'Silly old me!' said Ermintrude, laughing.

'It was never like this in the Hallé,' said Dougal. 'Get your hooves out of it!'

'No need to be like that,' said Ermintrude.

And Zebedee restarted . . . 'All together now,' he said.

Once again, they start to play . . .

'No! No! No, mam,' said Dylan. 'Follow the beat!
Please . . .'

Ermintrude promised to try harder and apologised for
holding them up.

'Fun though,' she said.

Zebedee, undaunted, tried again.

Brian is on top of a harp.

'Hey! It's a long way down, isn't it?' said Brian.

'Just play,' said Dylan.

'I'm stuck!' said Brian.

'Oh, man,' said Dylan.

'I don't think Brian's very happy,' said Florence.

'I'm stuck on a harp!' said Brian.

'Well, you would choose the harp, wouldn't you? Great oaf!' said Dougal.

'I think you're rotten!' said Brian.

Ermintrude was all for carrying on without the harp. So Zebedee said they'd better. 'Ignore all harp cues,' he said.

There's a crash of a drum.

'And drum cues,' said Ermintrude.

'How humiliating,' said Dougal.

Florence thought they should get on and so did Dylan.

Dylan falls over with a crash.

Ermintrude was prepared to give her all . . .

'I'm still stuck!' said Brian.

'Oh, what is the point of it all?' said Dougal. 'Come on, kitten on the keys,' he said, which made Ermintrude very cross. 'Get off.'

'Cheeky thing!' said Ermintrude.

Zebedee had one last try . . .

Dylan rallied round . . .

Brian solved his particular problem.

'I'm unstuck,' he said, 'and lovely with it.'

'I think a lullaby to finish with,' sighed Zebedee, 'as it's time for bed.'

Dylan, Sleepwalker

Dylan woke up and began to think about his life.

'Like . . . where am I going? Is it true what they say? Do I sleep too much?' said Dylan, falling asleep.

Dougal was having a little think as well.

'Now where's that rabbit?' said Dougal. 'It's got to stop. The time has come . . . *definitely*. I don't think I've ever once seen him leaping about like a rabbit. And what about all this hole digging he's supposed to do? Not one single hole dug in *years*. He's getting rabbits a bad name, that's what he's doing. Now I'm as tolerant as the next dog but IT'S GOT TO STOP! He'll be growing his hair next and . . . and . . . and . . .voting Liberal.'

Dylan's worries about his life were making him walk in his sleep . . . When he woke up and found himself on his feet he got more worried than ever.

I'm cracking up, he thought. Oh my! Oh my! Oh my!

'What shall I do?' he groaned.

Brian found Dougal pacing around the garden.

'You have a problem, little furry mate,' said Brian. 'I can tell by your nose.'

'You leave my nose out of this,' said Dougal.

Zebedee asked what the matter was.

'That rabbit,' said Dougal. 'He'll have to go.'

Dylan had decided that a few gentle exercises might

be a good idea . . . and perhaps a little sprint.

'All he needs is a little exercise,' said Zebedee. 'He should get a dog. Or . . . what am I saying?' He went to see Florence who was doing a few exercises too.

'They're worried about Dylan,' he said.

'Oh?' said Florence. 'I'd better go and see then.'

Dylan was still at it . . . Swimming, using a stool instead of water even though water would have been less hazardous.

CRASH!

. . . Shadow boxing, which he found even more exhausting.

And to prove it, he falls asleep and begins to snore.

'7, 8, 9, 10, out!' they said.

'Now what do you mean about my nose?' said Dougal.

'Well, when you get worried it twitches,' said Brian.

Florence asked Dylan if he thought the exercises were doing him any good.

'Do you feel any better?' she asked.

'Mam . . . I feel dreadful,' said Dylan. 'I'm beginning to think a person shouldn't try to change his natural way of life. And with me, sleeping is in, exercise is *out, out, out*.'

'I wonder,' said Florence.

'Now listen!' said Dougal.

'Oh man, spare me!' said Dylan. 'Can I help it if I'm naturally . . . like . . .lazy?'

'Now listen!' said Dougal.

But Dylan didn't . . .

'He's running!' said Dougal.

'You know, it's time for bed,' said Zebedee.

'You know, I could do with a sleep,' said Dougal.

'Touché,' said Dylan.

Spaghetti Party

Florence met Mr Rusty.

'Oh, you've brought me some flowers,' he said. 'How very touching.'

'Oh, I'm sorry,' said Florence, 'they're for someone else.'

'I knew they were,' said Mr Rusty. 'I was only joking. Who are they for then?'

'Dylan,' said Florence.

'Flowers for Dylan?' said Zebedee. 'He needs flowers?'

'He's invited me to a party,' said Florence.

Dougal was invited too. 'I wonder what's cooking?' he said.

'Greetings, guests,' said Dylan.

'What's cooking?' said Florence.

'It's a surprise, mam,' said Dylan. 'I hope you're going to like it.'

Florence gives Dylan the flowers.

'For you,' said Florence.

'Why, mam, you shouldn't have bothered,' said Dylan.

'I . . . er . . . didn't bother,' said Dougal.

'It's the *thought*, Dougal,' said Florence.

'Well, I thought I wouldn't bother,' said Dougal.

'I'm here! I'm here!' said Brian.

'Oh, bully!' said Dougal.

'Ermintrude,' called Florence.

'Here, dear heart,' said Ermintrude.

'Hello,' said Florence.

'Oh, I *am* looking forward to this, I'm so hungry,' said Ermintrude.

'She'll eat it all,' hissed Dougal.

'Do I hear a little doggy voice?' said Ermintrude. 'Speak up, dear boy.'

'Yes?' said Dougal.

'You're frightened I'm going to eat too much, aren't you, silly billy?' said Ermintrude.

Dylan said everything was ready and he hoped they'd like it.

'I wonder what it is,' said Florence.

'Ready?' said Brian.

'Surely,' said Dylan.

'Goody,' said Brian.

'Moo,' said Ermintrude.

Dylan hoped they weren't expecting anything too grand.

'Is this place in the *Good Food Guide*?' said Dougal, with a laugh.

Ermintrude asked Brian if he'd take her in to dinner.

'Delighted,' said Brian.

'Help yourselves,' said Dylan.

'Isn't he *sweet*!' said Ermintrude.

Dougal inspected everything.

'I wonder if there's a pudding,' said Ermintrude to Brian.

'I wonder if there's a pudding,' said Florence to Dougal.

Dylan asked them to sit down, so they did.

'Not *carrots*, I hope,' hissed Dougal.

'Ready, men?' said Dylan.

'Hope it's carrots,' said Brian.

'Do you?' said Ermintrude.

But it wasn't carrots – it was spaghetti. Florence tried some.

'Delicious,' she said.
'Er . . . excuse me,' said Ermintrude.
Dougal tried it . . .
'Good?' said Dylan.
'Very,' said Florence.

Brian starts to slurp noisily.

'Really!' said Dougal.
'Any more?' said Brian.
'I can spare a little,' said Ermintrude.

ABOUT THE AUTHOR

Eric Thompson was born on November 9, 1929 in Sleaford, Lincolnshire, and brought up in the village of Rudgwick in Sussex.

He trained to be an actor at the London Old Vic School and joined the company in 1952 where he met his wife, the actress Phyllida Law. Their daughters, Emma and Sophie, are both actors.

A founder member of the Royal Exchange Theatre in Manchester, he directed several plays there, in the West End of London, Washington, Broadway, Holland, New Zealand and Canada.

He first wrote *The Magic Roundabout* from his cottage in Argyll where he hoped to retire with a clinker built boat, a soft-topped jeep and a collie dog. He died in 1982.